CW00829664

Father Dolling: A Memoir

Father Robert Radclyffe Dolling

Father Dolling: A Memoir
Edited with an Introduction by Matthew Fisher

Joseph Clayton

ROBERT WILLIAM RADCLYFFE DOLLING was a social reformer and charismatic High Church Mission Priest. He was born on 10 February 1851 in Magherlin, in the North of Ireland. His Christianity was firmly Evangelical until he began working with High Churchman Father Stanton in St. Alban's, Holborn. Father Dolling is primarily remembered for his work at St. Agatha's, Landport, especially the Portsmouth Gymnasium and his 'manly' Christianity. Following his departure from the Mission he authored *Ten Years in a Portsmouth Slum* (1896). Dolling's first curacy was at Corscombe, Dorset, though he spent his time leading a Mission to the slums at St. Martins's, Stepney. Following a disagreement with the Bishop of London he resigned almost immediately after his ordination. Following a short break he took over the Winchester College Mission to the slum district of Landport, Portsmouth, resigning ten years later after another disagreement with a Bishop (this time the Bishop of Winchester). Dolling struggled to find a permanent position and travelled throughout England and North America leading missions, raising money and preaching. He was finally offered St. Saviour's, Poplar in 1898. He spent the next four years fighting for the residents in the East End, regularly preaching in West End churches raising money for his causes. He combined both love and a strong character and gathered around him a faithful group of helpers, including his sisters. He kept an open house and common-table throughout his ministry and spent his time loving the unlovable and showing them the God who he believed was able to save them. His work among thieves, prostitutes, schools, workhouses and drunk clergymen affected many lives in late Victorian England. He died after an illness at his sister's house in Earl's Court, on 15 May 1902.

JOSEPH CLAYTON (1868-1943) was a journalist and biographer. *Father Dolling: A Memoir* is his first book. His other works included further memoirs of High Church clergymen and the growth of the Labour movement. He was a Christian Socialist, converting from Anglicanism to the Roman Catholic Church in 1910. He was a friend of Robert Dolling for fourteen years and writes with compassion and a desire that Father Dolling would not be forgotten and that his love for mankind would be memorialized following Dolling's death.

MATTHEW FISHER studied History and English at university and is the webmaster of www.FatherDolling.co.uk, which remembers and promotes the work and life of Father Robert Dolling. He is interested in wider Ecclesiastical History, particularly eighteenth and nineteenth century Millenarianism. He is co-host of the *Hello Mormonism* Podcast and blogs at www.HelloMormonism.co.uk. His twitter is @fisherssomerset.

First Published in 1902 by Wells, Gardner, Darton & Co., London
Editorial material and Introduction Copyright © Matthew Fisher 2019.

First Printing: 2019

ISBN 978-0-244-74992-7

BREM Books UK
27 Goldcroft
Yeovil, Somerset, BA21 4DG

Front Cover photograph from Robert Dolling's *Ten Years in a Portsmouth Slum* (1896). Rear cover and inside photograph from Joseph Clayton's *Father Dolling: A Memoir* (1902).

www.FatherDolling.co.uk

Contents

Contents

BOOK FOUR: A WIDOW

Acknowledgements

I would like to thank my lovely wife Rachel and daughters Beth and Esther for their patience and kindness in showing some enthusiasm for the work of Father Dolling during this project. To Alastair Wilcox, who first introduced me to Father Dolling. Father Maunder, for being so generous with his time. My University lecturers, Sandy Braddick, Patrick Pender-Cudlip & Katy Limmer. With grateful thanks to the Portsmouth History Centre, Chris Richardson, Sue Ruston and Dave Mangles.

Introduction

Joseph Clayton wrote this short memoir of his dear friend of fourteen years (p. 9) shortly after Father Dolling's death. In 1902, it was hoped that Dolling's curate at St. Agatha's, the Reverend Charles Osborne, would write a "fuller and more detailed memoir" (p. 11). These hopes were realised when the 375 page *The Life of Father Dolling* was published in 1903 by Edward Arnold, London. In addition, Dolling's only published work, *Ten Years in a Portsmouth Slum*, was long out of print by the time Dolling died and Clayton hoped "perhaps [it may] be brought out again" (p. 124). Clayton's wish was granted in September 1903 when the sixth edition of Dolling's account of the work at Portsmouth was published. Whilst *Ten Years* tells the story of the Irish High Church slum-priest's incredible devotion to the poor people of Landport, this memoir encourages the reader to understand all Dolling's work and also his views on politics; the theatre and literature; the Boer War, including soldiers pay; his 'methods' with drunk Vicars; and even the issues of water supply to East London. Therefore, this short *Memoir* is more than a memorial to the deceased Father Dolling, it provides insights into many aspects of late Victorian city life and attitudes to a wide range of topics.

Dolling's religious devotion began at an early age. When he was only four years-old he found, for him, a sufficient explanation of the triune nature of his God. He stated "I've got meat, and potatoes and gravy on my

plate...that's three things. But it's only one dinner." (p. 20). His claim that this was "like the trinity" was applied during his ministry and undoubtably made him unpopular with some of the Church of England hierarchy. These conflicts were not limited to his High Church methods but included his belief in extempore prayer. Father Dolling combined Evangelical zeal in the God who loved the unlovable individual, with sensory ritualistic services accessible to uneducated people whom he desired to experience the love of the Infinite God. Perhaps in the same way that Dolling understood his God through the triunity of his dinner, the reader of Father Dolling, or other writing on Victorian poverty and religion may find enlightenment in the unity of the 'trinity' of work on Father Dolling[1], the 'irregular' slum-priest. It is this *Memoir* which, at the time of writing, is least quoted by historians. It is expensive to purchase[2] and is not available as an e-book[3] and therefore theologians and historians generally choose to study, if they study Dolling at all, *Ten Years in a Portsmouth Slum* and *The Life of Father Dolling*. Without doubt much can be gleaned from these publications, but it is in reading the 'trinity' of work that the fullest grasp of Father Dolling and his work is achieved[4]
.

---

[1] J. Clayton, *Father Dolling: A* Memoir (1902); R. Dolling, *Ten Years in a Portsmouth Slum* (1896); C. Osborne, *The Life of Father Dolling* (1903),

[2] On 03 January 2018 there were no copies available to purchase on Amazon.co.uk, and only two copies, both from the United States, on Abebooks.co.uk, both of which cost over £40 including delivery to the UK.

[3] This publication can be purchased as an e-book

[4] I would suggest that the *Memoir* is a great introductory text on Father Dolling and slum priests, then the specific work by Robert Dolling, *Ten Years in a Portsmouth Slum* should be read before Charles Osborne's *The Life of father Dolling.*

I was first introduced to Father Robert Dolling whilst reading a pamphlet on the Victorian church revival in Portsmouth[5], when my History lecturer entered the room and began discussing Father Dolling with me. I had not reached the section on Dolling in the pamphlet, but being a good undergraduate student, I confidently acknowledged I knew what he was talking about. I hurriedly began researching Father Dolling and wrote essays on the slum-priest, with my lecturer's warning that I would become increasingly sympathetic towards his work as I studied ringing in my ears[6]. Whilst studying, I visited the beautifully ornate St. Agatha's Church, Portsmouth several times.

Although Clayton records Father Dolling as never converting from the Church of England to Roman Catholicism (p. 162), in the 1990s St. Agatha's, the basilica which today is sandwiched between a car park and an arterial road carved through Portsmouth, integrated with the Roman Catholic Church. Father Maunder is the priest in Dolling's old church which is now a "member of the Ordinariate of Our Lady of Walsingham, under the patronage of Blessed John Henry Newman."[7]

Father Dolling's *Ten Years* is scattered with theology, politics, a liberal use of hyperbole as well as information regarding the social history of Landport and how Dolling believes problems are best fixed. It is this *Memoir* that helps contextualise this great religious leader and social reformer who loved the big picture but worried about small

---

[5] N. Yates, *The Anglican revival in Victorian Portsmouth*, (1983)

[6] I am a low church Nonconformist and was confident that this would not be the case. I was wrong.

[7] Information on St. Agatha's Church can be found at www.stagathas.co.uk

details (p. 42). His provision of the famous Clarence Street Gymnasium in Landport illustrates his understanding of what is required to change people's lives. Additionally, the approach and style of his contemporary Samuel Smiles is arguably visible in Dolling's text. Commonality between them is found with the inclusion of anecdotes and the belief that people must help themselves out of their own problems. However, they offer different solutions[8]. Smiles suggests religion as one of several solutions[9], whereas Dolling argues that only religion, particularly Christianity, removes the "nakedness of spirit" which leads to an improved life[10]. It is in the differing solutions to British Victorian society that Samuel Smiles and Robert Dolling part ways.

Historian Jeremy Morris identifies that "[m]any of those contributing to the literature on the revival era [of the High Church] are themselves Anglicans inspired by the revival, or friendly critics"[11] suggesting they should be understood as supporters of the work. Researching Dolling is therefore a challenge due to the limited availability of writing on the subject and the apparent low regard[12] for his mission and work. However, this challenge should encourage the reader to persevere because the information hidden in the works

---

[8] Compare S. Smiles, *Self Help with Illustrations of Conduct and Perseverance*, (1896), p. 1; R. Dolling, *Ten Years in a Portsmouth Slum* (1896), p. 132

[9] S. Smiles, *Self Help with Illustrations of Conduct and Perseverance*, (1896), p. vi

[10] R. Dolling, *Ten Years in a Portsmouth Slum* (1896), p. 23.

[11] J. Morris, *The High Church Revival in the Church of England* (2016), p. 1

[12] All three of the works on Dolling are primarily available in late nineteenth or early twentieth century 'original' editions, or facsimiles published as 'print on demand'. However, Matt Wingett (a Portsmouth writer) edited *Ten Years in a Portsmouth Slum* (2015) with a very short introduction.

are beneficial and applicable to twenty-first century society and religion. In making this *Memoir* available it is hoped that future work will be published so that Dolling and his mission may be understood as important to those who are undertaking study of late Victorian England and those who minister to the poor in Britain, and around the world, today.

Morris is a good example of an historian's approach to the work of Dolling and other slum priests with only a brief mention as an anomaly[13] whilst their work focusses on the broader High Church. Morris considers Dolling and others like him as part of the "post-Oxford movement legacy"[14] and discusses the myth of the slum priest. Additionally, Dolling was critical of the Oxford Movement (p. 160). This explains, in part, why his work is not traced through any contemporary Christian denomination. However, I suggest a link between early British Pentecostalism and the work of the slum priests. It is possible that the introduction of the welfare state in the early twentieth century meant that "Father Dollings" were no longer required and that the sensory Christianity of the slum High Church was re-expressed in the Pentecostal movements founded by the Jeffreys brothers.

Like Morris, Owen Chadwick[15] reduces Dolling to one of seven priests listed as "quality...priests who used the ritual" among the poor. Thus, no comment is made on the validity

---

[13] That is that the slum-priests require mentioning because of their Ritualistic services. However, they do not require exploration because they are seen as separate to the mainstream Oxford Movement.

[14] J. Morris, *The High Church Revival in the Church of England* (2016), p. 9

[15] O. Chadwick, *The Victorian Church: Part Two 1860-1901*, (1972), p. 312

of their work and only an acknowledgment that the work took place is referenced. The only other comment made by Chadwick is a comparison between Dolling and another priest, suggesting Dolling never read, because he claimed to have better things to do with his time than read books[16]. This is at best an exaggeration of inferences made by Dolling and Osborne and is disputed by both Joseph Clayton (p. XX44) and Alastair Wilcox[17].

Wilcox also quotes Dolling without evaluation, which could suggest Dolling is utilized to confirm Wilcox's work on Liverpool. However, when he discusses the lack of spiritual fruit of St Agatha's gymnasium, he suggests Dolling was "worried that his Portsmouth club did not yield ecclesiastical return"[18]. Yet Dolling justifies the great benefit of the gymnasium, writing an emotional response to his critics, who measure success only in terms of ecclesiastical results[19]. Dolling's 'manly' Christianity, expressed at a time when "Christian Piety...had been a 'she'"[20] illustrates that Dolling and others offered counter cultural expressions of Christianity. Perhaps, this is one of the main values of reading Robert Dolling from a theological perspective. Truly, there are parallels between twenty-first century expressions of Christianity and the late Victorian period.

In addition to the above, historians' treatment of Father Dolling and the changes to the demography and topography of Landport may offer an explanation for the lack of interest

---

[16] O. Chadwick, *The Victorian Church: Part Two 1860-1901*, (1972), p. 175.

[17] A. Wilcox, *The Church and the Slums* (2014), p. 109

[18] Ibid. p. 184.

[19] R. Dolling, *Ten Years in a Portsmouth Slum* (1896), p. 31.

[20] C. Brown, *The Death of Christian Britain* (2001), p. 196..

in Father Dolling. Without doubt Dolling's mission-work in Portsmouth is the primary focus of Dolling's life and Clayton devoted the greatest proportion of this memoir to that work. Landport is no longer a residential area, having become rundown in the early twentieth century before sustaining considerable bomb damage in the Second World War, subsequently being demolished to be replaced by car parks and a shopping centre. However, the church of St Agatha's remains, and Dolling continues to be memorialised by the priest in charge, with the church being restored in the likeness of Father Dolling's description found in *Ten Years*.

Robert Radclyffe Dolling believed in an experiential Eucharist, stating "nothing...but the Blessed Sacrament"[21] can bring men to a faith-building supernatural meeting with the real Jesus Christ. However, there are limitations for historians when researching people such as Dolling. When their stories are written they are often recorded by some of their closest supporters, means finding an account which is critical of the subject is limited to gleaning nuggets of negative information from a broadly supportive writer. At the time of his death newspapers[22] relied upon Dolling's own writing of *Ten Years* to produce an obituary. Even St. Agatha's curate's account of his "dear Friend Robert Radclyffe Dolling" was compiled at the request of Dolling's family[23]. This is supported by Nigel Yates who writes, regarding Dolling, "[t]he historian is forced to rely entirely on the contemporary publications, which are either essays in self-vindication, or biography of the most hagiographical

---

[21] R. Dolling, *Ten Years in a Portsmouth Slum* (1896), p. 199-200.
[22] 'Father Dolling Dead' (1902) *St James's Gazette*, 16 May, p. 6.
[23] C. Osborne, *The Life of Father Dolling* (1903), p. vii

type"[24]. Therefore, any historical investigations regarding the late-Victorian Landport Mission are limited because of the information available. It is true that this *Memoir* is a supportive work, but we must not think that it is therefore without worth. It is for this reason that this new edition of *Father Dolling: A Memoir* is being made available now.

Much was written relating to the ecclesiology and charismatic character of Father Dolling. For example, the High Church nature of the opening ceremony of St. Agatha's is discussed in detail by *The Evening News*[25], describing the use of incense, crucifixes, flowers around the altar and Dolling "engaging in prayer and elevating the Host, indulging in many genuflections all the while". At the time of his death one newspaper stated, "there were thousands that day who felt that in him they had lost their best friend on earth"[26]. These characteristics were evaluated by Booth, who argues that success of High Church missions was because the lives of people leading them "were more evidently self-denying, their enthusiasm more forceful"[27]. Yet little research has been focused on the theological stance of Dolling, beyond the reason he left Landport and his connection to ritualism. In fact, Father Dolling's theological stance was more nuanced than the simplistic representation of a High Church slum priest. His roots were in Irish Evangelicalism (or Protestantism) (p. 23) and this was amalgamated with High Church practice whilst he was still a Deacon. Dolling never lost his

---

[24] N. Yates, *The Anglican Revival in Victorian Portsmouth,* (1983), p. 9.

[25] 'New St. Agatha's' (1895) *The Evening News,* 28 October, p. 1.

[26] 'The Late Father Dolling' (1902) *The Devon and Exeter Gazette,* 22 May, p. 4.

[27] In O. Chadwick, *The Victorian Church: Part Two 1860-1901,* (1972), p. 312.

Evangelicalism but found a fuller expression of his God when High Church and Evangelical conviction both played their part in the salvation of individuals.

Robert Radclyffe Dolling relied on Osborne being a theologian because he felt he was not[28]. Readers should note that "the Bible was his great book" (p. 121) and that he was widely read, including having a love of Charles Dickens and others. However, Father Dolling's belief in "the power of prayer, the power of repentance and the power of the Sacrament"[29], meant Dolling promoted an experiential Christianity that affected a person's sense, demanding a response which reaffirmed the individual's belief and feelings. For example, during a church service in Mayfair he spontaneously called for the people to get on their knees and pray for South Africa. This form of Christianity was anti-intellectual, placing it at odds with Evangelical Christianity of the late nineteenth century. Additionally, Dolling hints at a more Charismatic theology, though caution should be taken as Dolling repeatedly uses hyperbolic statements throughout *Ten Years in a Portsmouth Slum*. His purposes for writing included the need to raise £2290 to pay debt he owed to the mission[30]; a plea for continuity in the school and children's services[31]; and to explain his reason for resigning whilst justifying his work in Landport[32]. Additionally, Dolling is repeatedly thankful to those individuals who have been involved in the successful ministry at St. Agatha's. However, this *Memoir* ends at the death of Robert Dolling; the concerns of this

---

[28] R. Dolling, *Ten Years in a Portsmouth Slum* (1896), p. 158.
[29] R. Dolling, *Ten Years in a Portsmouth Slum* (1896), p. 193.
[30] R. Dolling, *Ten Years in a Portsmouth Slum* (1896), p. 184;240.
[31] Ibid. p. 51;56.
[32] Ibid. p. 171.

world are no longer his concern and it is those who are left behind who must continue to promote his memory, lest he be forgotten.

Perhaps Dolling, in addition to Roman Catholic practice, aligns himself with Pentecostal and Charismatic theology by stating there is a type of "faith that works miracles of healing today"[33] and, when discussing a blind man's abilities suggests he must have learnt from a supernatural source. These show Dolling's search for a marrying of the theological and the experiential. The introduction of "Extempore prayers"[34] and a belief that "praying" has "more potential than giving"[35] adds evidence to Dolling having a Charismatic theology. However, Dolling's thinking appears separate to that of certain modern Charismatic movements because his theology is primarily Christocentric. In fact, it is Dolling's sermon-like justification of his soteriology, showing the centrality of "[t]he compassion of Jesus Christ" being experienced through the "Blessed Sacrament"[36] which not only aligns him with Roman Catholicism but also the Charismatic movement. Therefore, Dolling's ministry could perhaps be viewed as a predecessor to the Pentecostal revival of the early twentieth century, having more in common with the Charismatic renewal of the 1960s and liberal Christianity than the Oxford Movement, which Dolling saw as unsuccessful because of "its initial peculiarity 'that it was made up out of books'"[37]. This meant it did not have the

---

[33] Ibid. p. 118.
[34] Ibid. p. 154.
[35] Ibid. p. 52.
[36] Ibid. pp. 198-200.
[37] C. Osborne, *The Life of Father Dolling* (1903), p. 169.

experiential element that Dolling felt had the power to save the individual.

It is with sadness that Clayton notes Dolling was "never really happy at Poplar" (p. 132) and yet his devotion to the people was beyond question. He fought for his flock and those outside of the church who lived in Poplar. In 1901 he "begged" a remarkable sum of over £5,000 by preaching in churches in the West End to raise money for the East End Mission.

His difficulties with Bishops are recorded in this *Memoir*. Portsea priest Father Bruce Cornford "who knew and loved" his fellow minister declared Father Dolling's ministry "a powerful indictment of the stupidity of Bishops."[38]

One of the great difficulties in researching Father Dolling is that historical events are recorded by people with a vested interested in the promotion of the people involved.

Much more could be said about Dolling's physicality in ministry but without doubt, many people to whom Dolling ministered desired to live a better life and benefitted from Dolling's charisma. Rather than viewing Dolling as part of a subsequent generation of the Oxford Movement, perhaps he should be lauded not only by Anglicans and the Roman Catholic Church, but also by the Charismatic Movement and the liberal church, as a great reformer in both ecclesiological practice and a life of love poured out towards the poor.

---

[38] Father Bruce Cornford was curate in the Church of the Holy Spirit, Portsea during Dolling's ministry in neighbouring Landport. It is in his copy of C. Osborne's *The Life of Father Dolling* that he has handwritten the above statements. His signature inside the front cover and handwriting have been compared to available records of that Church during the late nineteenth and early twentieth century.

A re-evaluation of Father Dolling would be beneficial from a theological, practical and historical perspective. Therefore, it is hoped that this *Memoir* will stir the reader to think about this much neglected, apparently selfless slum-priest who "was so human, and...had been killed with work" (p. XX47). Truly it may be said of him "Greater love has no one than this, that someone lay down his life for his friends"[39].

Matthew Fisher, 2019

---

[39] John 15:13 (English Standard Version)

Further Reading

Works Relating to Father Dolling

Roger Bryant, *Don't Touch the Holy Joe* (Rowlands Castle: Ragged Right, 1995).

Robert Dolling, *Ten Years in a Portsmouth Slum* (London: Swan Sonnenschien, 1896).

Desmond Morse-Boycott, *Lead, Kindly Light* (London: The Century Press, 1932).

Charles Osborne, *The Life of Father Dolling* (London: Ed ward Arnold, 1903).

Neil Yates, *The Anglican revival in Victorian Portsmouth* (Portsmouth: Libraries, Museums and Arts Historical Publications, 1983).

The High Church & Oxford Movement

Owen Chadwick, *The Spirit of the Oxford Movement* (Cambridge: Cambridge University Press, 1990).

Shane Leslie, *The Oxford Movement 1833-1933* (Milwaukee: The Bruce Publishing Company, 1933).

Jeremy Morris, *The High Church Revival in the Church of England* (Leiden: Brill, 2016).

Bernard and Margaret Pawley, *Rome and Canterbury: Through Four Centuries* (Oxford: AR Mowbray & co., 1974).

Walter Walsh, *The Secret History of the Oxford Movement* (London: Swan Sonnenshien, 1899).

Studies on Religion

David Bebbington, *The Dominance of Evangelicalism* (Leicester: inter-varsity Press, 2005).

David Bebbington, *Evangelicalism in Modern Britain: A History from the 1730s to the 1980s* (London: Unwin Hyman, 1989).

Callum Brown, *The Death of Christian Britain* (London: Routledge, 2001).

Owen Chadwick, *The Victorian Church: Part Two 1860-1901* (London: SCM Press 1972).

R. P. Flindall, ed., *The Church of England, 1815-1948* (London: SPCK, 1972).

S.J.D. Green, *Religion in the Age of Decline* (Cambridge, Cambridge University Press, 1996)

Walter J Hollenweger, *The Pentecostals* (London: SCM Press Ltd, 1972).

Hugh McLeod, ed., *European Religions in the Age of Great Cities, 1830-1930* (London: Routledge, 1995).

Jeremy Morris, *Religion and Urban Change: Croydon, 1840-1914* (Woodbridge: Royal Historical Society, 1992)

Keith Thomas, *Religion and the Decline of Magic* (London: Penguin Books, 1971).

Alastair Wilcox, *The Church and the Slums* (Newcastle upon Tyne: Cambridge Scholars Publishing, 2014).

S.C. Williams, *Religious Belief and Popular Culture in Southwork c. 1880-1939* (Oxford: Oxford University Press, 1999).

A Note on the Text

The following text has been retyped by Matthew Fisher from a 1902 First Edition of *Father Dolling: A Memoir*. What follows is the complete text, found inside the memoir with the same photograph of Father Dolling placed after the title page. The following text intends to remain faithful to Clayton's original spelling, capitalization and punctuation. Any errors are entirely the fault of the editor.

The original contents page (p.7) is reproduced as per the 1902 publication. However, due to the page numbers being different from the original publication, they have been removed to avoid confusion. A full Contents page can be found before the 'Acknowledgments' page. The footnotes on pages 26 and 49 are as per Clayton's 1902 text.

In reproducing this text, and making it available for purchase, it is hoped that the work and mission of Father Dolling may be further enlightened.

FATHER DOLLING

Father Robert Radclyffe Dolling

FATHER DOLLING

A Memoir

BY

J. CLAYTON

WITH A PREFACE

BY

HENRY SCOTT HOLLAND
CANON OF ST. PAUL'S

LONDON
WELLS GARDNER, DARTON & CO.
3, PATERNOSTER BUILDINGS, E.C.
AND 44, VICTORIA STREET, S.W.

1902

TO
THE MEMORY OF
ROBERT RADCLYFFE DOLLING
IN THE NAME OF

ALL THE FRIENDLESS AND SOLITARY WHOM HE
BEFRIENDED
THE OPPRESSED WHOM HE SUCCOURED,
THE HUNGRY WHOM HE FED THE SICK WHOM HE
HEALED
THE DEAD WHOM HE RAISED

CONTENTS

FOREWORD

This memoir has been compiled that some account, however inadequate, of the life-work of Robert Radclyffe Dolling may be in the hands of people before the memory of that rare and remarkable work grows dim.

As far as possible, I have quoted Dolling's own words from sermons, lecture, speeches. Letters, and talks for the story of his activities; and Mr. Dolling's sisters, Miss Blair, the Rev. A.H. Stanton, the Rev. J.H.R. Abbott, and others have given me many particulars of fact; but I alone am responsible for all matters of opinion, which are based upon a friendship that extended over fourteen years. The reader must forgive the shortcomings of this memoir; it has been so hard to write with the heart still aching at the loss of the man we loved.

I am grateful to Canon Scott Holland for his preface, and I hope all who read this little book will do what they can for the memorial to Father Dolling. The real memorial is in the lives of men and women whom Dolling delivered from misery; but there ought to be something substantial standing in his name.

J.C.

OWLPEN, NEAR DURSLEY,
    GLOUCESTERSHIRE.

PREFACE

We cannot better discover the power of personality or the impotence of words than by trying to convey to others, through report, the vivid impress of a strong soul that has passed out of our sight. Yet this is what we are driven to attempt, and this little book gallantly set itself to the impossible task.

Those who knew and loved Father Dolling cannot let the felt pleasure of his presence pass away without an effort to express to others that which to them meant so much, and all who have shared the joy of this experience will be glad to have it set down at once while the memory is keen and the affection undissipated, that they may say over to themselves the tale that they cannot bear to forget.

A fuller and more detailed memoir – by his intimate friend and colleague, C.E. Osborne – we hope may appear later. In the meantime, here is put down the immediate impression of the man as we remember him at the moment that he is taken from us.

The man! For with Father Dolling it was the man who was one with the evangelist and the priest. It was his absolute self, in its characteristic identity, and not merely some incidental gift or outlying sentiment, which was made the instrument for the Divine use. He told for God through being what he was, and the personal equation was inseparable from his work. He had his methods and his

11

principles, and he thought them out, and he could put them into words. But, still, to explain the results, you must say, and could only say, 'It was Dolling.' He would have made anything tell. He had the gift to let his innermost personality come through and speak.

That is what the Winchester boys became aware of, in spite of all that held them aloof from the type of man, so strange to them, and from his ways of working, so unintelligible to most, and so repellent to many. Suddenly, as he spoke to them, they would catch sight of his soul ablaze: the light kindled, the passion and the pity, the hope and the love of the Gospel broke out through face and lips. They knew now, and some for the first time, what religion meant. They gave themselves away to it. The real thing was there, whatever the odd ritual in which it disguised itself, and they meant to stand by it, whatever freaks it indulged in. That prolonged hold on the confidence of Winchester, whether of masters or boys, was the highest tribute that could be paid to the simple force of Dolling's personal religiousness, just because it was won over those who are, perhaps, of all living beings, the most remote from the special form of spiritual work which Dolling embodied.

Our British public school-boy – we know him. Our British public school-master – him, too, we know. And we know, moreover, the curious type of worship peculiar to public schools, with its quaint pre-historic condition, unlike anything else on the face of the earth, and its terror of anything that commits it, or of anyone who should let himself go. Winchester is typical of all that is most rooted in our public-school tradition. Yet it never failed Dolling. It trusted, believed, backed him from first to last. The men who came out of the school stood by him, worked with him still, however remote they were from his standpoint of practice. It was enough that it was Dolling. They were convinced that he had hold of the secret, and could do what he was set to do – win souls for Christ out of the slums. And they were convinced of this because they themselves had known something of his power over their own souls. Of course, there was also the discovery made that he could enter into their school-life with a boy's own inwardness and apprehension. He made himself their mate; he sat in their rooms and talked; he brought into play that burly *bonhommie* of his, the robust joyousness of the 'jolly Friar,' the love of buoyant and natural life, which was so deep in him. And, then, he had a very shrewd, practical judgment: he understood men and things, and boys and masters; and he got inside the business in hand with a sound and thorough common-sense which they had not expected in a parson. He could steer them in a 'row' round a difficult corner. He could mediate between opposing forces. He saw matters on their level, and yet could introduce something of authority into his opinion. He was very human, very large-hearted, very tolerant of all natural feelings. He would come to the business in hand without any narrow *partipris*, and, above all, without a touch of pose or priggery. The school-boy found himself interested; and what did it matter, then, how much Dolling was given to rum goings-on in his church? He was all right: he was a 'decent chap' – could praise go higher? And just what told on the public-school, or the Magdalen men, as he drew them toward their school or College Mission, told with equal force within the Mission itself. He knew perfectly well how identical is the Gospel which really goes home upon the soul at every level of social life. There is but one strange message it speaks, and practically in the same words, to educated and uneducated, to bond and free. So Dolling's power over his people came through the personal impression of his evangelical convictions. He kept the whole fabric of his worship alive through this quickening spirit of 'conversion.' This book will tell of his free speech and open prayer. He allowed no mistake to be possible about where the root of the matter lay.

Religion, after all, must be religion; it must mean a spiritual life, a converted will, a humble and a contrite heart, a love of God and of man. He let nothing overlay these or compensate for the lack of these. He had, indeed, a certain body of Ritual Practice, more or less elaborate, and very definite in its intention. And he appreciated beautiful ministration. But the secret of his work lay behind or underneath this. He insisted, indeed, strongly on the Sacrament of Penance and Absolution; but, then, this was to him an essential element and agent in the process of conversion. He pressed the central dominance over all worship of Eucharistic adoration; but, then, the Sacrament of the Altar was to him the Spirit and the Life. He could not conceive a division between the inward and the outward manifestation of God's Pardoning Grace. Evangelical and Catholic Truth found here for him their perfect fusion, in the hunger of the forgiven soul for the Body and the Blood present in the Bread and the Wine.

All this he needed to have emphatic and pronounced, without disguise or modification, if his vivid missionary attack was to be possessed of its obvious completion. His inward message could not bear to be deprived of its outward expression, and he was angry at any cautious check put upon him, yet not so much with the Ritualist's ecclesiastical anxiety, as with the missioner's indignation at being thwarted in his Gospel.

But if his strong personal character told upon public schools and upon his missions as an attractive and compelling power, it had one special field in which it put out all its particular force. He could sway and hold the outcast and the broken in a way and with a freedom that were all his own. Here, in this region, the personal equation is bound to be at its highest. The waifs and strays of social life can only be reached through flesh and blood, through a masterful individuality, through a living present affection, through the touch of an intense personality. So only can the incredible become credible, and the impossible be made a fact.

The book will doubtless tell fully of the adventures, and risks, and losses, and glories that belong to work done with such unstinted generosity, and such open-hearted confidence. Dolling was determined to keep the road back home open to those who but loved too fondly the ease of the 'open road.' House and table, room and companionship, were to be theirs when they chose. Let them walk in and find it.

Nothing but his steady and shrewd wit, his firm will, his human common-sense, could have made it all possible. But with him the risks could be run. Those who were everybody's despair could have their chance given them here. It was exactly what we most need in these terrible cities, that sweat and break men, body and soul. Here was the moral hospital, the spiritual home of convalescence. Here was the House of Rest, with large open-air treatment, and strong meat for those who could take it. It was the rarest of all gifts that Dolling revealed. He had that passionate sympathy with Bohemianism and Prodigalism which let him inside the hearts of the men to be won; but he combined with the firm, wholesome judgment that never lost hold of the sanities of the soundness of moral well-being. He had glimpses in the secret of the soul, which disclosed the amazing heart of goodness and of sacrifice and of pity that can be found behind all the sinful disguises of Publican and Harlot. Somewhere in them there is the hidden, which if only it can be unearthed or quickened by the violence of the Divine Compassion can put to shame all the righteousness of the ninety-and-nine. And even in its sin it can often disclose touches of the self-sacrificing passion which finds its full expression in the Cross of Christ. This he believed, this he had the gift to verify. It is in this that he taught us most and gave us his best, and is now most sorely missed.

With such a force of individual character, who could be surprised if he had his rubs and tumbles? With his temperament, with his spontaneity, with his confidence, with his masterfulness, he was bound to bump up against the ordinary hum-drum fashions of men.

No one who ever saw his stout square head, his bull-neck, his burly presence, could doubt that he would give things a jolt or two that would make them jump.

A man cannot have such gifts for nothing. He must pay the price. Some of it may be his own fault; some of it – a great deal of it – will be the fault of a puzzled world, of a startled Church, of bewildered Officialism, of conventionalized Parochialism. We can leave others to do the sum and work out the total of respective guilt.

But no one can expect to possess abnormal gifts, and yet to find their exercise perfectly smooth in a world that of necessity bases its calculation on the normal.

No one can have the supreme boon of originality and yet find himself instantly understood and appreciated by those to whom he must, on this very hypothesis, be a surprise and a shock. Originality has got to establish its right to exist; the abnormal has got to make good its function and use. And this will never be done without some suffering in life of which sacrifice is the vital law.

Let no one who has the glory of the gift complain of the price that he pays for its possession.

We have, surely, lost something in our day of the old Tractarian patience, which never dreamed of a success to be achieved straight off, but took the suspicion and distrust that it aroused as the natural portion of all who are charged with a special mission. They simply bided their time, and it arrived.

Looking back at Dolling's career, I cannot lift a loud wail. He had two moments of trouble, one at leaving the London, and one at leaving the Winchester, Diocese. But he had unparalleled confidence reposed in him by his supporters, and enthusiastic support almost from the very first. Never did anyone more rapidly win the devotion of those who believed in him. He was given a golden opportunity even while he was a Deacon. He got Magdalen College at his back, and Bishop Walsham How. And then, after an abrupt flinging over of the work in London, in consequence of a blunder of his Bishop, which he took to heart with, perhaps, over-hasty indignation, he found himself in possession of that wonderful confidence of Winchester School, which never failed him for those long, good years under Bishop Thorold.

He had come to the end of what he thought it was given him to do in Landport when the collision with the Diocesan so unfortunately clouded the close. Then came two years of real anxiety lest his Church should fail to trust and use him again, during which interval his American friends, by their splendid and gallant generosity to him, did their utmost to bribe him away from his home allegiance. Chandler, the present Bishop of Bloemfontein, had the honour of wiping out of discredit by offering him the work of St. Saviour's, Poplar, in which he died.

He found it hard to fight against the apathy of that London which had won his first love, and he had a weary work of begging to do; but he put his whole heart out for the children, and found in them his solace and his hope, while his old power of witchery won him immense support from outside.

He was hard at it when he died.

It is ours to see to it that his memory shall live, to tell what Christ's Priesthood may do in this Church of ours for Christ's own poor.

He showed us how pitifully we cramp the worship of Grace and narrow the range of the Gospel within out limited traditions and ecclesiastical timidities. He shocked us out of our nervous proprieties, and taught us to plunge and hazard and dare on behalf of those of whom we despair, but for whom Christ sets us to seek.

He proved to us how much could be done if we only committed ourselves heart and soul to that which we profess, and let the strong message that is on our lips have clear and free way.

He showed us what the Book of Common Prayer could do, and what it could not do.

He stormed against our frigid conventionalities, and shook our Anglican self-esteem.

We recognised through him how often we had taken pride in what was in reality our insular limitations.

He stretched and strained our tethers, not in a spirit of disloyalty, but in the fretted impatience of a workman who found himself hampered by the formalities and qualifications in the very task he had been commissioned by his Church to fulfil to his Lord.

He demanded first place for the poor; he bent his ministerial charge to their primal needs; he strongly claimed for them their right to social and civic amelioration.

This book will, it is hoped, recall enough to show how real and full was his Gospel.

The Catholic movement will yet continue to move, if only it is embodied in those who, like Robert Dolling, root their Priesthood in Evangelical conviction, and carry it out in its demands over the full range of social human life.

H.S.H.

FATHER DOLLING

A MEMOIR

CHAPTER I

BOYHOOD AND YOUTH

ROBERT WILLIAM RADCLYFFE DOLLING was born in Magheralin, County Down, on February 10, 1851. His father, at one time High Sheriff of Londonderry, was an Englishman. It was his mother – a daughter of the late J. Dupres Alexander, M.P., and niece of the first Earl of Caledon – who was Irish, and from her he first learnt of the religion to which he gave his heart. Robert took to religion from infancy, lisping words of prayer and hymn at the age of three, exhorting and preaching to his sisters long before he had learnt to read. The baby theologian never missed an opportunity of putting in a word for religion. At the age of four he startled the dinner-table by 'explaining' the doctrine of the Trinity, which some grown-up person had declared to be very difficult of understanding.

'I've got meat, and potatoes and gravy on my plate,' Master Bobbie remarked – 'that's three things. But it's only one dinner. That's like the Trinity.'

When he was six years old, at a children's party, during a pause in some theatricals, Bobbie was asked to conduct a lady to the piano and request her to sing, whereupon he suggested gravely: 'I think we had all better sing the 100th Psalm.'

One anecdote of childhood is quite characteristic of the parish priest who kept open house at Portsmouth and Poplar.

On his fourth birthday Bobbie was lying dangerously ill. He woke up in the evening, remembered it was his birthday, and asked where his cake was. When it was brought he said: 'It ought to be cut up, and everybody must have a piece, and those in the kitchen as well.'

'Those in the kitchen' were always to be included in his hospitality and fellowship.

Of saying prayers and putting on his night-gown to preach to his sisters, the child Dolling was never tired. But he was not fond of study, and it was not till he was nine years old, and had been for six months a pupil at Mr. Seagar's school at Stevenage, that he really learnt to read. He loved to be read to, and his memory was extraordinarily retentive. He would get his sisters to read over to him the little reading-lessons they all studied in the old Mavor's spelling-book, and then, having got them by heart, would in his turn recite the legends of 'Ann Cox' and 'Frank Pitt.' He thought it a better way than struggling to spell out the lessons for himself.

In 1859 Robert was sent to the preparatory school at Stevenage, and he left there at fourteen to proceed to Harrow. Dr. Butler was Headmaster of Harrow at that time, and Dr. Farrar, the present Dean of Canterbury, was Dolling's class master.

The religious precocity of his childhood had already developed in Robert Dolling into a strong sense of duty to

God. He went through the ordeal of an English public school with his standard of personal purity flying high, and the unsavoury vice that disfigures the school life of so many, and is bemoaned so bitterly in secret, left the soul of Robert Dolling unscathed. He was in Vaughan's house first of all at Harrow, and afterwards in Bull's, and so exceptional was the strength of his character, and so great his influence, that he was always put in the rooms of bad repute; it was recognised that Dolling never allowed vice to go on, and his presence expelled the common evils of school. The strength and tenderness that characterized Father Dolling the clergyman were in the Harrow school-boy, and the love of little children that drew them to him in the crowded streets of Portsmouth and Poplar took him often to Mrs Vaughan's nursery at Harrow. All that is remembered and told of Dolling's school-days show a boy of rare and exalted purity – strong in mind and resolution. But strength of body was not in those days, and until the age of twenty Robert Dolling was constantly ailing. A weakness of the eyes gave him a lot of trouble, and hindered very seriously his studies. At Harrow he never distinguished himself in scholarship, and when he went on to Trinity College, Cambridge, he was quite unsuccessful at examinations. Dolling liked to describe himself as 'an unlearned man,' who had never passed his 'little go'; but his lack of health told seriously against book learning, and he only stayed a year at Cambridge.

It was in his undergraduate days that Robert Dolling met the Rev. H. A. Maconochie, and visited the Church of St. Alban's, Holborn, of which Maconochie was vicar. Dolling's religious sympathies were drawn at once to

Maconochie and to the famous 'ritualistic' church in Baldwin's Gardens. The conspicuous devotion of the clergy in what was then and is still a slum parish, a devotion that has kept those three clergymen, the Revs. A. H. Stanton, E. F. Russell and G. R. Hogg, at St Alban's for over twenty-five years – Mr. Stanton has been at St Alban's for forty years – and the persistent persecutions of the church, met with splendid, unflinching unconcern, appealed to Dolling irresistibly. He liked the services and the social work carried on by Maconochie and his staff, and his fighting instincts went out to a church that was for so long the object of legal attacks. Though he had been brought up in the Orange atmosphere of Ulster Protestantism, Dolling took to ritualism and the Catholic doctrine of the sacraments instinctively; in many respects he was evangelical, believing intensely in the need of personal conversion, but his faith in the Holy Communion – the Mass, as he always called it – and in the Confession came to him as young man, and remained with him till his death. It was Bishop Forbes, of Brechin, he made his first confession about this time.

Dolling left Cambridge to assist his father, at that time land agent to the Mercer's Company in County Derry. It was not till some time later that he came to London for good, but during those years in Ireland he was constantly conducting Bible-classes for young men, and in Dublin he gathered round him a band of workmen, and turned his rooms into a common club-house for them. Mr. Dolling's relatives had moved to Dublin from the North of Ireland at that time, and he was often back there, even after he had left for London. The Bible-classes of those days were a very real thing, and in a touching resolution passed by the Select Vestry of Kilrea, County Londonderry, when the news came of his death, 'the chairman requested to write to Misses Dolling and to the clergymen in charge of St. Saviour's, Poplar, and to convey all-inadequate expression of the intense sorrow felt by everyone in Kilrea who still remembers "Master Robert's" life of active Christianity and practical benevolence during the years in which he dwelt amongst them; and to say further that several members of the Select Vestry present at this meeting had had the great privilege and benefit of attending his classes long ago, when as a layman he had taken immense trouble to elevate and enlighten and help the young people of the neighbourhood.'

At Kilrea, 1868-70, 'Master Robert' had Saturday and Sunday classes and night-schools and sang in the church choir. He continued his night-schools till 1875.

There are many photographs of 'Master Robert' at the period – Dolling liked to be photographed with a group of his boys around him – and they are the portraits of a young man of keen spiritual life. Occasionally he was photographed in the regalia of some political lodge.

At Dublin Mr. Osborne – then a student at Trinity College, and afterwards curate at St. Agatha's, Portsmouth – first met Dolling at a breakfast in Canon Travers Smiths Vicarage. 'I felt at once,' Mr. Osborne writes, 'that I liked him immensely – in fact, after about half an hour's conversation we seemed as intimate as if we had known each other for some time.'

Dolling was then mostly in London, but business matters often brought him to Ireland, and from Mr. Osborne we get a description of his life in Dublin:

'He built a set of rooms behind his house at Mountjoy Square, Dublin, and there he gathered round himself a sort of family of young fellows, who met on certain evenings during the week for recreation – either gymnastics, cards, or singing, or simply for a chat and a pipe with "Brother Bob," for the name given him by the London postmen had followed him to his Dublin home.... On some nights religious meetings were held in a little improvised chapel, but religion was never forced, and the line of the place was as removed from the Young Men's Christian Association as it was from that of a public-house. The mental atmosphere was essentially healthy and natural, and the influence of Robert Dolling was that of a young man with young men; not, as might easily have been the case with a less strong personality, of a prig with a band of parasites as disciples. Everything was thoroughly healthy and manly, as well as unselfish and affectionate, and many a lad in barracks or behind the counter was glad of "Brother Bob's" friendship, and of the privilege of spending the evening with other fellows, where there was at once no evil temptation and no stilted religionism.'

In 1878 Dolling, who then had money of his own, came to London, and the Rev. H. Maxwell introduced him to the clergy-house at St. Alban's, Holborn. The Rev A. H. Stanton was his friend at once. They were both enthusiasts, ardent democrats in politics, men consumed with love for their fellows, sacramentalists, determined to preach Christ's Gospel, and to show the Light of the World in the dark places of the Metropolis. Dolling cared nothing for the Establishment; he had only very moderate respect for church dignitaries, and he despised the common honours of success. He saw that the ordinary round of church services and the respectable family life of the average Church of England clergyman did not and could not touch the great masses of people in London and elsewhere, and he was not at all afraid of being thought unconventional. So Dolling threw himself into the work that Mr. Stanton had set going, and became 'Brother Bob' to the Brotherhood of Jesus of Nazareth and to St. Martin's League – the Postmen's Social Guild started by Mr. Stanton. 'Brother Bob' was not set on being ordained at that time. He recognised that as a layman he had more freedom. No priest was less trammelled by his office than Father Dolling was, but, still, there were things that could be done without offence by 'Brother Bob' that were practically impossible for a clergyman.

He gave himself heartily to his postmen friends of St. Martin's League, and lived as the Warden of the South-East District in the League House in Borough Road[1]. Some members of the League were rather annoyed when Brother Bob took to inviting into the house all the roughest lads of the neighbourhood. Postmen must be scrupulously clean, and there was so much vermin in the house after the lads had been in. But they loved Bob, and learned to put up with his ways. His sympathy and single-heartedness bore all before him.

Stanton was his very close friend in those years. Once they spent a month's holiday together in Ireland, staying with Dr. Alexander, the Protestant Bishop of Derry,

---

[1] St. Martin's League had several houses in London – clubhouses for post-office servants, where food, rest, and recreation were provided. Father Stanton only resigned the presidency of the League last year.

and with Dr. Logue, the Catholic Bishop of Raphoe. They came back convinced that Home Rule was an imperative measure of justice, and that the simple goodness and piety of the Irish peasantry could never be moulded to accept the commercial morality and consequent prosperity of England.

After some years' work as a layman at St. Alban's, Brother Bob's private resources came to an end – through the depreciation of land in Ireland – and an income of sort was necessary. Stanton advised him to be ordained and get a curacy. There was no question as to Brother Bob's call to religious life. He was then thirty, and all his life he had been preaching Christ – in his own way. Ordination would mean submission to the authorities of the Church; he would be no longer the free-lance he was as a layman, but would be under the orders of Bishops. There was much of the rebel in Brother Bob. The social injustices around him, and the calm complacency with which these injustices were regarded by the rulers of the Church and the State, provoked him to speak harshly of dignitaries. But if he was not ordained, he would have to go into business, and that would keep him from the work his heart was in – the work of strengthening the weak, comforting the forlorn, feeding the hungry, and binding up the wounds of the broken humanity around him.

Brother Bob could not leave his work to make money in business, and so he went to Salisbury Theological College to spend two years preparing for ordination.

CHAPTER II

ORDINATION – THE MILE END MISSION

OF course, 'Brother Bob' could not be satisfied with the study of divinity at Salisbury Theological College. He was never a 'bookish' man, though he had a strong taste for good literature, but was distinctly a man of action, loving people more than books, and finding them more interesting. So at Salisbury, in the intervals of lectures and study, he spent his time at a little mission church in that city – a mission dedicated, like the Postmen's Guild and the little chapel of his first curacy in East London, to St. Martin.

Dr. Moberley, the Bishop of Salisbury, and the principal of the college, the Rev. E. B. Ottley, were both very kind to 'Brother Bob,' and with Mr. Ottley's aid he managed to get through the college course, and to pass the Bishop's examination for the office of deacon.

Then came the question of curacy. 'Brother Bob' wanted to be in London, but it was customary for Salisbury theological students to spend their first curacy at least in Salisbury Diocese. Bishop Moberley had the wisdom to recognise in Dolling a man of unusual gifts, and so an unusual course was adopted. Mr. Sowter, afterwards Archdeacon Sowter, was the Rector of Corscombe – a little Dorset village – and he proposed to take Dolling as his curate, and to pay him the necessary salary. At the same time Mr. Sowter was interested in a small East London mission church in the parish of Holy Trinity, Mile End, and it was to this East End mission church that Dolling was chiefly to devote himself. Dr. Jackson, the Bishop of London, Dr. Walsham How, the Suffragan Bishop of Bedford, as he was called, whose diocese was East London, and Bishop Moberley, all agreed the plan, and so on Trinity Sunday, 1883, Robert Radclyffe Dolling was ordained deacon in Salisbury Cathedral.

Very few sermons were preached in Corscombe Church by the new curate; before the end of the year he was far too absorbed in the work of his St. Martin's Mission at Mile End to have any time for Dorsetshire, and Mr. Sowter raised no objection.

Holy Trinity, Stepney, is a large parish, and Dolling found it necessary to insist that his corner of it, St Martin's district, south of the Mile End Road, and with a population of 8,000, should be quite independent of the control of the Vicar of Holy Trinity. Bishop Walsham How admitted the force of the plea – there were personal reasons that made it impossible to work with the vicar – and St. Martin's District under Brother Bob was in all respects a separate parish – only there was no income attached to it – owing allegiance to the Bishop alone. It was a remarkable position of responsibility for a newly-ordained deacon to be in, the sole charge of a populous district at the East End, a poverty-stricken and neglected district; and that an ordinary youthful, inexperienced curate should be placed in such a position is unthinkable.

But Dolling was then a remarkable man, and he was thirty-three – ten years older than the average newly-ordained – and he had had very considerable experience of men and of life. He set to work at once to make his little mission chapel and clubroom in Maidman Street – Just off Burdett Road – a centre of light and of healing. He had great ideas of a famous church to be one day erected there, a church that should be 'exceeding magnifical,' and of clubs that should be built. St. Martin's Mission should become, if it were permitted, an East-End cathedral, a social settlement – human, not academic – and a palace of joy for God and the people, not given up to technical classes. Slums, crime, and poverty should vanish before the coming of the Light. Democracy would remove the economic and political distress, and Christ's religion would renew the manhood and womanhood of East London and build up character in the new era. Miss Elise and Miss Geraldine Dolling and Miss Blair helped him in those days at Maidman Street, as they helped him later at Portsmouth and Poplar. His enthusiasm drew lots of men from Magdalen College, Oxford, to support the mission, and for two years the good work went on.

'Brother Bob's' intense personal religion, his belief in humanity, his rare sympathy, and his utter fearlessness made the St. Martin's Mission quite different from anything else in the Church of England at that time. Night after night he would sit in his club-room in an atmosphere reeking of tobacco-smoke, surrounded by dockers, soldiers, and costers, playing cards, leading the chorus of a popular song, or superintending a boxing match. Nothing came amiss to him, nothing shocked or dismayed him. The eight thousand people round him were his children, his brothers, to whom he was 'Brother Bob' or 'Father' Dolling. How he came to be called 'Father' is not known; he was not then a priest, and certainly had no ecclesiastical right to the title, and St. Martin's Mission was never a prey to those ritualistic young persons who like to style every high-church clergyman 'Father.' But the East Enders called him 'Father' just as the old dwellers in the slums of Holborn called Mr. Stanton, of St. Alban's, 'Father'; the press confirmed the title, and 'Father' he remained. We have many pictures of the days and nights at St. Martin's Mission: of the open house, frequented by 'mothers in the afternoon, children in the evenings, boys and men at nights'; of Brother Bob in cassock and biretta 'enthroned on the top of a table, amid clouds of tobacco-smoke, sitting in judgment, and hearing all kinds of little domestic causes'; of the common supper to which 'a motly crowd of parsons, undergraduates, soldiers, newspaper boys, burglars, vagrants, and anybodies' sat down. The mission buildings were not extensive – a club-room downstairs and a little chapel in the upper room had to suffice. Dolling never could regard his house as a private residence, still less as the Englishman's 'castle'. It was an essential part of his religion to share all he had with his friends and neighbours, and his friends were often the outcast and the felon, and his neighbours the wounded and stricken whom he found fallen on the wayside. He had no sense of personal property, no lust of possession, no mania for owning things. Even his bed he would give up when some poor tired body needed it, and sleep on the floor in his sitting room. Dolling's house was always 'home' for waifs and strays, the vagrant and homeless.

And with this genial, human good-fellowship, this sympathy, this social brotherhood, there was other work to be done: money to be begged for carrying on clubs, for food and raiment, for the immediate relief of some of his 'children'; many letters to be written; tickets for hospitals and convalescent homes to be obtained; sick people to be visited. There were services, too, in the little chapel – six services every Sunday – and many sermons to be preached. And the vitality of the place and the work was Dolling's religion. The strength and beauty of his character drew men and women to him. Without his deep spiritual life the social work at St. Martin's would have been just as flabby and unreal as most of the philanthropic and social work in East London and elsewhere is. Lots of well-meaning people, inspired by Dolling's work, have tried to conduct clubs on his lines, and when the experiment is unsuccessful, they shake their heads over 'the ignorance, apathy, and ingratitude of the working classes.' But Dolling's inner life, his constant communion with the Unseen, his oneness with his God, was the secret of his successful social work. His religion was not an attitude of mind, not a duty to be fulfilled, not something extraneous: it was his very self. Every morning he knelt in prayer at the altar, in prayer that could not be framed in well-balanced sentences; every morning in the quiet and peace he listened to the voice of his God, held communion with the Infinite God of the universe Whom he worshipped, and found in the contemplation of the life of the Son of Man in Galilee of old the ideal life for all the sons of men. The spirit of God was in him in those hours of communion and all day. In the strength of that spirit he could enter public-houses, drink and smoke with his fellows, and draw them to a cleaner and more temperate life. He knew the needs of his east London neighbours, knew their weaknesses, their privations, and became on with them because he was one with God. Without the realization of the unity of life – or, at least, of the oneness of humanity – and of a Divine Light illuminating all the children of earth, the social reformer and philanthropist is generally a hard or priggish person; and the religionist who neither knows nor loved his kind, be he ever so devout, is not likely – we have it on the authority of Holy Writ – to know or love God.

In Dolling the love of and belief in the spiritual, the unseen, were as strong as the love for the belief in mankind. And so Brother Bob walked those dingy streets off Mile End Road, Maidman Street, Edwards Road, Wentworth Road, Forrester Road, and Bridge Street, and sat in the crowded club-room with his boys, a man of power and character, a personality – a friend to whom one might tell the story of failure and crime, whose compassion would never be shocked at any confession of sin and folly, but not a man with whom a liberty might be taken. There was something about Dolling that made the thought of a liberty, of any offensive familiarity, impossible. He was 'Brother Bob,' he was the mate and 'pal' of the coster and the gaol-bird, the friend of all publicans and sinners; but he walked the earth with a dignity that came of fellowship with God, and in the slum, and at the smoking concert, or at the bedside of some poor, dying woman, Robert Dolling carried with him a presence that convinced. It was character that told all the way through with Dolling, and his character was built up by the free play of the Spirit of God, by a communion with Eternal Truth that left no room for the petty failings, the self-esteem and jealousy, that commonly disfigure. The sense of humour that carried him through so many minor trials came of this communion. Because he was pure in heart, because his heart knew no corrupting thought of personal honour, glory, or riches, he saw God; and seeing God and the Truth, it was impossible to be worried or seriously cast down at disappointments that would have broken of embittered the spirit of many another man in his place.

And so for two years, from 1883 to 1885, St. Martin's Mission flourished. Men crowded into its club-room, and a room was found for a boys' club. Three times a week meals were provided for the children of the neighbourhood; the Miss Dollings gave shelter to poor girls of the street; the Father succeeded in getting ten bad houses closed; boys just out of gaol or off the street were housed at the clergy house and given a fresh start; nearly two hundred other boys were emigrated, or had work found for them; the little chapel was crowded to overflowing every Sunday. And all the time Dolling was only a deacon, and therefore disqualified from conducting certain services of the church. He could not celebrate the Holy Communion himself, but had to depend on the help of priests in the neighbourhood, and he could not receive confessions in his official capacity, nor declare absolution. His daily work left little time for the theological reading necessary for the passing of the examination required by the Bishop for all who sought the priesthood, and it was not till Trinity Sunday, 1885, that he was ordained priest in St. Paul's Cathedral by Bishop Temple. In the immense congregation that filled the cathedral on that Sunday morning in May were a large party of East-end mothers, who had travelled up to St. Paul's in two special omnibuses chartered for the occasion, to do honour to their friend and clergyman, 'Brother Bob.'

Dolling had quite made up his mind that upon ordination as priest the new license he would receive from the Bishop should not place him under the Vicar of Holy Trinity, Stepney, in whose parish St. Martin's Mission was situated. He understood that as he had been directly under the authority of Bishop Walsham How from his first coming to Mile End, so this new license would state his independence of Holy Trinity. He looked forward to the creation of a fresh parish for St. Martin's; and though content to wait till this could be accomplished, and to continue under the Bishop of Bedford, he was not content to be licensed curate of Holy Trinity, Stepney – to serve in a capacity which guaranteed no security of tenure, and which left him at the mercy of a summary dismissal at six months' notice.

To his amazement and intense disappointment he found that Dr. Temple had licensed him, after all, to Holy Trinity. Dolling felt there had been a breach of faith – that Dr. Temple, the new Bishop of London, had not taken the trouble to consider the needs of the little district off Burdett Road, and that it was impossible to carry on St. Martin's Mission unless its minister had a free hand. Could he stay on under the circumstances? Money was wanted; a new church was wanted, for the little chapel above the club was crowded out every Sunday; and a second clergyman was wanted. Money could be got, for Father Dolling was already an expert beggar, and over three thousand pounds had been begged in the two years, but there was no fixed and regular income for St. Martin's. A new church would have been the property of the Vicar of Holy Trinity on its completion, and a second curate would only have been licensed to the parish church. All the hopes and plans of Brother Bob were thwarted and frustrated by the denial of parochial independence. He felt he must resign at once. His conception of the Church made it impossible for the Mission to be outside the Church of England – his loyalty to the Church was never shaken by his conflicts with the episcopal authorities. He held the Church of England to be a Divine society, and that the validity of its sacraments depended on its Apostolical succession; and though he worked with Nonconformists, who did not share this belief, and avowed his admiration for their evangelical work, this conviction remained unaltered all his life.

But his work at Mile End was done. It was not only that the refusal of the Bishop to recognise St. Martin's Mission as a separate parish had made its growth and life impossible: Dolling's health was failing, and his doctor had declared, 'Overwork and want of actual necessaries have brought you so low that much longer at such work and you would cease to work at all.'

He did not speak harshly of the Bishop's action. He wrote to his friends, when a successor had been found for Maidman Street: 'I have the greatest respect for the Bishop of London – I believe when he knows his diocese he will rule it most magnificently. I have the greatest love for the Bishop of Bedford – I believe every energy and power he possesses is lavished on East London. But I believe neither of them know anything of the needs or wants or special

36

circumstances of Holy Trinity, Stepney;' and he urged them to support their new minister.

The foundations Brother Bob had laid in Maidman Street were not destined to be built upon by others. No one could carry on the work – the fact that St. Martin's Mission was tied to Holy Trinity made its position a very difficult one. The clubs dwindled and were closed; soon the little chapel was closed. And to-day, though the old buildings still stand in Maidman Street, nothing indicates to the passer-by that in this dingy street nearly twenty years ago Father Dolling served his first curacy. London populations quickly change, but there are still men and women in the streets of Burdett Road who remembered Brother bob and the old clubs, and his preaching in the upper room, and the wonderful sympathy of his sisters.

The announcement of his resignation fell heavily on the district. Men wrote to the papers and appealed to the Bishop, but nothing came of the protest. Dr. Temple was not the man to relax his authority or alter his methods because an East-End curate's work was upset. The sun streamed down on Mile End in those hot June days of 1885, but a shadow was on the hearts of the people. They hoped against hope that 'the Father would stay on , and when they knew he was really leaving them for good, they did the only thing they could to show their love, collected from their poverty a little money, and bought a few presents – a meerschaum pipe for Father Dolling, a silver bracelet for each of his sisters.

The last Sunday of his ministrations passed, the last sermon was preached in the little chapel, the last pipe smoked in the club, the last blessing given to his 'children,' a last shake of the hand with the tramp, the coster, the gaol-bird, and all the weary and heavy-laden folk of that little quarter of East London, a last word of comfort from Miss Dolling to her girls, whom she had restored to womanhood, and then the doors of the Mission, which had stood open night and day for two years, were closed, and Father Dolling, sick in body and with great sorrow on his soul, was gone.

Rest was the immediate thing he needed, rest before the next call should come to him and so he went to St. Leonard's-on-Sea, with the sound of the tears and blessings of the people he had served ringing in his ears.

CHAPTER III

PORTSMOUTH AND WINCHESTER

A few weeks at St. Leonard's-on-Sea brought some measure of new health and strength to Robert Dolling. Then came the call to Portsmouth. Winchester College had established a mission – St. Agatha's – in the slums of Landport, and the Rev. R. Linklater had been the clergyman in charge. In the summer of 1885, Dr. Linklater accepted the vicarage of Holy Trinity, Stroud Green, and upon his resignation of St. Agatha's, Dr. Fearon, the Headmaster of Winchester, offered the appointment to Robert Dolling. Bishop Walsham How was anxious that Dolling should have work, and several old Wykehamists at Magdalen and New College, who had looked in on the St. Martin's Mission at Maidman Street, wanted Dolling for the School Mission at Portsmouth. Dr. Harold Browne, the Bishop of Winchester gave his consent to the appointment, and in August, 1885, the matter was settled, though it was not till September 29 that the new missioner took sole charge of St. Agatha's.

The preliminary interviews with headmaster and Bishop were both memorable. The charm and strength of Winchester, and its simplicity, its unity and its solidity, were revealed to Dolling as he sat in Dr. Fearon's study, and he felt that the Landport Mission must be first among the school missions in England. From that day and for ten long years his love for the great public school that had called him to Portsmouth was a constant spur to increased activity and constant encouragement to renewed effort.

Dr. Harold Browne received him kindly at Farnham Castle, told him of the needs of Portsmouth, promised him the liberty that had been enjoyed by his predecessor, and hoped that he would not do anything foolish in his new sphere of work. Unfortunately, the good Bishop did not offer a night's lodging to the Winchester College Missioner, and as it was too late to get a train home, Dolling was obliged to pawn his watch to pay for a bed at an hotel.

Dr. Linklater introduced Dolling to the Winchester men, and they took to him at once, and remained his friends.

The story of the 'Ten Years in a Portsmouth Slum' has been told in a book that has obtained, and deservedly obtained, a very wide circulation. Yet the whole story of Dolling's work at Portsmouth is not written down in the 'Ten Years,' and can never be recorded by human pen. We can tell of his political and social work, we can describe his services in church and the life in St. Agatha's parsonage, but we can never really express the full significance of the patient daily ministry of those years at Portsmouth.

The district of St. Agatha's in 1885, bounded by the Dockyard Wall, Unicorn Road, Edinburgh Road and Commercial Road, and with Charlotte Street cutting through it, with its six thousand people, its fifty pubic-houses and fifty brothels, its sailors population, its riotous license, its open disregard of the decencies of civilization, its shrill gaiety, its poverty, its thieves and prostitutes, its savagery and heathenism, might have discouraged a braver spirit than Robert Dolling. He was still a young man, and at the age of thirty-five he had been bidden to preach the Gospel, to feed the hungry, to clothe the naked, to heal the sick, to visit those in prison, and remove stumbling-blocks from the ways of little children, in this dark quarter of Landport. It was a heavy responsibility and a big undertaking, but Dolling never refused responsibility, and he liked big things – details worried him sometimes, the planning of large schemes he enjoyed.

Those ten years at Portsmouth were the great period of Dolling's life. His sisters, Miss Elise and Miss Geraldine Dolling, Miss Blair, Miss Rowan and Miss Wells were with him all the time at St. Agatha's, doing for the women and girls of the parish what the clergy did for the men and boys. The Rev. C. Osborne was his curate for seven years, and when Osborne left the Rev. W. Dowglass, another Irishman, took his place, and shared the ministerial work.

How much the Mission owes to these seven people cannot be expressed. No man had more faithful and devoted helpers.

The area of the Winchester College Mission is not large, but it is very thickly populated, and while the Town Council had spent a good deal on the improvement of Southsea, Landport had been left untouched for fifty years. Its streets were badly lit, and vice stalked openly through the district. There were nineteen slaughter-houses in the very midst of St. Agatha's parish, boys ate raw meat and drank blood, and children made toys of the refuse of the slaughter-house, and fashioned their games on the killing that was always before their eyes. The public-houses were everywhere, and cheap sing-songs and concerts brought large numbers of people, men, women, girls and boys, to spend their evenings within these places of entertainment – with disastrous results. The churches made no attempt to touch the neighbourhood, the brewers grew rich upon it, the publicans lived on it, the prostitute plied her trade unhindered in it. Four little unattached Mission Halls, conducted by pious Dissenters, endeavoured for years to bring religion to the district, but did not prove interesting to the inhabitants. Dolling always spoke warmly of these efforts, and thanked God for their continuance.

Dr. Linklater and the clergymen who worked with him were not long enough in Landport to grapple with the savage heathenism of the place.

On the first Sunday afternoon of Dolling's ministrations at St. Agatha's, a shower of stones greeted him in Chance Street, and he saw with dismay some of the children on their way to church watching with interest two girls, whose only clothing was a pair of sailors trousers each, dancing a kind of breakdown with two young sailors, who had nothing on except the girls' petticoats. One couple, rather more drunk than the other, toppled over, and it was a movement on Dolling's part to pick them up that provoked the stones from the bystanders. On that same Sunday, later in the afternoon, at the children's service in church, two boys calmly lit their pipes and began to smoke, and when the new parson did the only thing that seemed possible to him – seized them by the back of the neck and ran them out of church, knocking their heads together on the way – the offenders, with their mothers, poured out such a volley of obscene abuse at the church door that Dolling was compelled to close the service hurriedly. He returned to his lodgings, followed by the two swearing women, and a crowd of children.

So the pastorate began.

Three years later Dolling could say: 'We have broken down all barriers between us. I believe everyone in the Parish looks upon us as their real friends. They are very glad when we call upon them; many of them are very glad to spend the evenings with us; there are no words called after us now, no stones thrown at us.' And ten years later, Sunday morning, October 27, 1895, a great precession of choristers, acolytes, and priests, all in their robes and with Dr. Ridding, the Bishop of Southwell and founder of the Mission, and churchwardens, and innumerable friends, passed through the streets, nearly blocked by a crowd, at once respectful and affectionate, to take possession of the new church – the new St. Agatha's, the massive basilica raised by the energy of Robert Dolling and the devotion of his friends. The church stands to bear witness to that craving of the children of earth for the worship of the Infinite, the desire to find and know God. In the Landport slums there were many to whom St. Agatha's brought light and life; many poor souls found in its services comfort and peace from their daily troubles, found strength to endure day after day the hardships of privation, assurance in their loneliness that God cared for them. In the quiet of the early morning in church in simple faith they found their God and communed with Him, as men communed with God in the earlier ages of the world. All arguments of the rationalist against this religion, all warnings of the Protestant against the superstitions of Rome, beat vainly against the people who worshipped at St. Agatha's. They found God there, found him Whom they sought (as the religious-minded must always find what they seek); they talked freely with him, and passed from the church to the overcrowded rooms where they lived, to the factory and dockyard where they worked, stronger and braver men and women. St. Agatha's parish has not been converted to the Christianity of the Church of England; only a comparatively small number of its inhabitants ever worshipped in the old church, and only a small number worship in the new, though it has been opened these seven years. But from time to time man in his weakness seeks the Eternal, seeks some outward manifestation of the Divinity that shapes his ends, longs for a God Whom he can know and worship, and often finds in church and sacraments a revelation of his God. And so St. Agatha's Church in the Landport slums is a memorial of man's dependence on the Infinite. Its usefulness is not to be measured by the number of its communicant members, nor the size of its congregations. There were many who came but rarely to the church to whom it gave vision of other worlds than that of commerce, to whom it recalled the story of the life of the Man of Nazareth, to whom it stood constantly for a Justice and Charity wider then current conceptions of these things. Landport does not follow the call to prayer when the bell rings, but the church often makes passers-by pause, and involuntarily their thoughts are directed to the Infinite God, Whom Father Dolling served. If our churches stand empty amid the rush and scramble of the workaday world, still they point to the Christ-life, and promise a Peace of God. And if Father Dolling's parishioners at Landport were not drawn in great numbers to the church by his preaching, yet he brought a new life and hope to the multitude around him, and the Mission and the church will always be associated in the minds of Portsmouth people with the message of fellowship and justice, that Dolling's religion brought to Landport, the memory of a brave man who strove for ten years with the powers of evil to make his parish a cleaner, sweeter place.

At. St. Agatha's Dolling could say that after a year he was fast getting rid of the bad houses in his parish, and could tell of clubs and a gymnasium established.

After five years' work, he wrote:

'We have put into the Army 39 men, into the Navy 57 men; we have emigrated to Australia, America, and elsewhere, 63; we have started in life over 100 young men who have lived with us; we have reformed 25 thieves just out of gaol; we have sent to service and into shops about 100 girls; 25 girls have passed through our training home, staying from four to two years – there are 19 in it now; we have turned many drunkards into respectable church-going people; we have rescued 144 fallen women and got them into homes, and we are maintaining in preventive homes 124 girls and boys snatched from the brink of ruin; we have shut up in the district over 50 brothels; and have changed the whole aspect of the place; we house 6 old couples free of rent; we feed for a halfpenny a time 180 children and 25 old people free twice a week during the winter; we teach over 500 children in our Sunday-schools and about 600 in our Day-schools.

And before ten years had gone by the old church was found too small for the people who attended, and the new church was opened.

Dolling hated statistics, and knew the danger of measuring progress by the counting of heads. Yet he kept account of all whom he prepared for confirmation during the ten years, and the number stands at 580 – more than half of whom were over twenty. Nearly 300 of these left the parish for the colonies, the army, the navy, or the grave, but 202 remained members of the Communicants' League, and did not desert the church when Dolling left.

St. Agatha's Church was only a part, and not perhaps the chief part, of Dolling's work at Portsmouth. He was a member of the School Board and Board of Guardians, and his labours on those bodies, and on political platforms, and at public meetings, are recorded in other chapters. His influence in the town was very great, and all sorts of people valued and trusted his opinions.

Then there were many visits to Winchester, for within a year Dolling was writing that it was a very wonderful thing how he, a stranger, had been allowed to enter, as it were, into the very life of the school, staying in College, in Commoners, and in Houses. He had been able in the that short time to get to know personally all the masters and many of the boys, and to count many friends among them. Once a week he went regularly to Winchester in term time, arriving for mid-day dinner, spending the afternoon watching cricket or football, enjoying the hospitality, the friendliness, the generous atmosphere of the school. The perfect relaxation of that weekly holiday literally kept Dolling alive. Often he went to Winchester despondent and ill, and in an hour or two he had laid aside both sorrow and sickness. The school did much for Dolling. What did Dolling do for Winchester? It was not his business to preach to the school, except on a few rare occasions; his mission was to Landport. Loyalty to the Winchester authorities forbade any conscious attempt to exercise a religious influence in the school. No Winchester boy was drawn to join the Mission at Portsmouth, or to seek ordination through Dolling's influence. Still less was Winchester attracted to ritualism or to auricular confession. Every week some of the older boys visited St. Agatha's and attended the services, and returned to Winchester a little mystified by the ceremonial they had seen on Sunday – the incense, the vestments, the postures of the officiating priests and acolytes – but quite content to believe that Dolling knew best what was wanted at Landport, and not at all desiring such services for themselves. It was not in religious matters that Dolling's influence told on Winchester, though many a boy was helped through dangerous and difficult periods of school life by his timely word, and many an old Wykehamist treasures some saying of Dolling's that has stood him in good stead in after-life. The influence was mainly social; it made the boys less exclusive. It opened their eyes to another world than that in which they lived, a world of hard manual labour, a world of poverty – bitter, abject poverty – a world of misery and distress. They had heard of this world, of course, but with Dolling at Landport they entered it, and found that it contained men like themselves, human and cheerful, bearing burdens with a patient dignity before which even a public-school man could only bow his head.

As for the money that Winchester gave to the Mission during the ten years first and last, it must have amounted to nearly £40,000. The people of St. Agatha's subscribed over £4,700, church societies gave £1,800, and the bulk of the rest of the £50,904 subscribed for St. Agatha's came from Winchester – from old Wykehamists, and from parents, masters, and boys. The Mission was a striking object-lesson on the voluntary principle in Church matters; it is not a matter for surprise that Dolling cared nothing for the Establishment. St. Agatha's bore witness to the fact that where people want a church the means are forthcoming for church and minister – for the erection of a magnificent church and for a minister who always wanted money for rebuilding schools, for clubs, for the purchase of houses for parochial purposes, and for a thousand and one charities.

The relations between Winchester and Dolling were always cordial. Dr. Fearon and the Wykehamist committee trusted him absolutely, and this generous confidence made an enormous difference to Dolling's work. He felt that he could appeal to Winchester at any time of need. Once when the Mission was at its last gasp for money, and Dolling was thinking that he would be obliged to pawn things, he wrote to each House Master at Winchester, asking him to tell the boys after prayers on Sunday how terribly straitened matters were. By Wednesday morning £33 15s. had come in, and Dolling knew that it came from the men themselves, because they had not had time to write home about it.

Of course, some of the Winchester men thought it not quite right that the Mission should be always in debt, but even then they felt that Dolling must be allowed to go on in his own way at Landport, and somehow the debts always did get paid.

Sometimes Dolling had a reminder that Winchester was not always thinking of the Mission. He used to tell a story of how he once asked a little boy what he should preach about in the little boys' chapel. The boy answered, 'The first week men are here they spend nearly all they bring in grub. Then in the middle of the term their pitch-up[2] generally send them something, and they spend that in two or three days. And then in the last two days of term they spend the extras of their journey money. Now, I would advise you to tell men' – and Dolling thought he was going to say that they should give some of this waste to the starving people at Landport – 'that it would be much wiser for them, and they would enjoy themselves a great deal more, if they portioned out their money week by week.'

Dolling enjoyed the Mission work at Landport. He always declared it was much easier and pleasanter than an ordinary parish clergyman's work, because it was so much more hopeful. 'Faith in humanity is the foundation of all mission work,' he used to say, 'and it is very easy to be attained in a slum, where every single day some soul reveals progress; but it is hard to keep such faith alive in a parish where your church is well filled by a respectable congregation.' Besides this faith in humanity, Dolling always pointed out the great need there was for continuous intellectual development in those who worked in slum quarters. He knew the temptation to accept the problem of poverty as a matter to be solved by immediate relief of distress, and, even when absorbed in a multitude of philanthropic agencies, urged upon all who would listen to

---

[2] 'Pitch-up' is Winchester for parents and home.

49

give greater attention to the underlying causes of social misery.

Of course, there were many battles at Landport, tough struggles with civil and ecclesiastical authorities. There was a fierce contention in 1894 with the Mayor concerning the state of Portsmouth – a matter we shall refer to elsewhere. Then there were attacks by certain Protestant organizations upon the ritualistic character of the services at St. Agatha's and remonstrances from Bishop Harold Browne and Bishop Thorold – remonstrances that never affected Dr. Harold Browne's protecting support of the Mission, nor diminished Dr. Thorold's very real affection for Dolling and St. Agatha's. Both these Bishops disliked a great deal that was said and done at St. Agatha's, and Harold Browne could never bring himself to visit the Mission; but both knew the heathenism of Landport, and were thankful for the work that Dolling did. Dr. Thorold visited St. Agatha's, and stayed at the Parsonage, and his visit made the Mission very dear to him.

In March, 1890, there was a great scare in Portsmouth that Dolling was resigning, and prayers were offered in many Nonconformist chapels that the Winchester College Missioner might be retained in the town. The trouble was a very simple one. The Rev. Stewart D. Headlam had been invited by Dolling to give one of a course of Lenten addresses in St. Agatha's, and, of course, Mr. Headlam preached on Christian Socialism. There was nothing in the sermon different from what Dolling and Osborne often preached, by Dr. Harold Browne, Canon Jacob, the vicar of Portsea, and the Warden of Winchester College were all seriously disturbed by it, and when Canon

50

Jacob and the Warden wrote withdrawing their support from the Mission in consequence of Mr. Headlam's address, Dolling felt that Winchester was against him, and sent in his resignation. But Winchester wouldn't hear of his resignation, and the Warden explained that he only wrote in his private capacity, while the Bishop strongly desired Dolling to stay.

Of all the complaints made against St. Agatha's, not one ever came from the people in parish and not on ever came from Winchester.

Dolling's last struggle with the Bishop of the Diocese was in 1895, and it ended in his retirement from Landport – a retirement he had desired twelve months before, but which he had decided to postpone for a year or two, in consequence of the opening of the new church. Dr. Thorold died in 1895, and Dr. Randall Davidson was made Bishop in his place. Dolling informed his new diocesan of the plans made for the opening of the new St. Agatha's Church in October, and of the kind of services held in the church. The Bishop found himself unable to sanction some of these services, and proposed that they should be brought into 'harmony with the Prayer-Book.' Dolling at once sent in his resignation, and it was accepted. Dolling felt he could not alter the services he had been conducting for eight years. He knew that all round him clergymen, high church and low, were disobeying the rubrics of the Prayer-Book without episcopal reproof. Dr. Davidson had never visited Landport; he could not understand the needs of the place as the Winchester College Missioner understood them. It seemed to Dolling that to yield to the Bishop would be to acknowledge that one had been wrong, and that Dolling could not admit. He believed his services were the right thing for Landport, and that the Prayer-Book was made for man, and not man for the Prayer-Book.

Dr. Davidson and Dr. Fearon both regretted the resignation. To the Bishop and to a large section of the public it seemed unreasonable to leave for what appeared to be a small matter of difference. But to Dolling it was the condemnation of his work that he saw, and it was impossible for him to acknowledge that the Bishop knew better than he did in dealing with Landport. To stay on was to admit the right of an outside authority to interfere with St. Agatha's – it seemed better to go. An affectionate request from the Bishop Dolling would have obeyed, as he obeyed the requests of Dr. Davidson's predecessors; but the Bishop wrote as a Bishop concerning the church services, and Dolling resigned.

The new church had been opened in October, On December 9 the letter of resignation was sent in, and then, after a month of fruitless endeavour to prevent the Missioner leaving – the saddest and most mournful month that Landport ever knew – came the final good-byes, and on January 11, 1896, Father Dolling and his sisters left Portsmouth for good. He left his people with blessings on his lips, and with no word of bitterness. As he had come to Landport a poor man, so it was as a poor man he left. But many buildings remain as fruits of the ten years' work; and as the money had been poured out freely for these temples of human artifice, so had Dolling freely poured out the treasures of his great love on Landport; had poured out himself heart and brain for the building up of the immortal in men and women, for the stablishing of a kingdom of God not made with hands, lasting beyond the claims and controversies of time.

CHAPTER IV

ST. AGATHA'S PARSONAGE

To get any sort of real impression of the ten years' work at Portsmouth, it is necessary to understand the part played by the open parsonage house. The open house and the common table were, in Dolling's mind, essential in the work of Christian Mission; they were to him what a surpliced choir, a daily church service, or a new altar cross were to the fervent high-churchmen of an earlier generation. After nine years' residence in Landport, Dolling writes:

'The chief expense of the Mission remains – the cost of my own house; but every day it proves to me conclusively that this is the most useful work we do. Our Mission, I believe, is the only one in England that aims at a common table. Every day one feels that common food is a true and real sacrament between men, and it is wonderful how a house like ours adapts itself to every use.'

From the beginning of Dolling's ministry St. Agatha's Parsonage was open to all who needed help in body or soul, to all who wanted to learn to heal. First of all he lived in Spring Street, but the arrival of three lads from Mile End, and the visits of Winchester men and other chance guests soon left no room. For two or three nights Dolling was obliged to sleep in the bath-room, and when the bath was wanted as a bed, he slept on the landing outside. The

Parsonage was overcrowded throughout, and it was absolutely necessary to move in to Chance Street. But things were not much better here, and we get a glimpse of the state of things in 1887 in one of Dolling's Annual Reports:

'Of course, we need more buildings. My own sitting-room, where I write, make sermons, read, see people, and rest is the common room of the Parish; it is never empty. Two dear ladies sent me a sofa this week, with the proviso that I must not let it be used by our rough boys. I fear it will have to go to my bedroom – that is the only unintruded place; but that means an extra fire, and we have to study economy, and cannot live yet like average work-people, for our house has become really the Parish Home. All kinds and sorts of people come to stay with us – our Winchester men, our old London boys, clergy, Members of Parliament, soldiers and sailors on furlough, and officers, thieves just out of prison, sometimes even a stray Lord. Then our Parish people come in at all times, and our meals to suit all this have to be of the simplest. We ask a great many sick children, and some men out of work, into dinner and tea. As I write this a sailor is playing a fiddle, and there are about fifteen fellows dancing and singing. It does not conduce to clearness of intellect, but it is very homely.'

But even this house Dolling felt ought to be given to his sisters, whose work in the parish was of the very first importance, and so he moved again into a wretched cottage next door to the Gymnasium in Clarence Street. Then it was only by turning a large upper room of the Gymnasium into a dining-hall that the common meals could be continued. The walls of the cottage were damp, the floors rotten; it was very cold in the winter, and, of course, there was no room for the usual number of guests. Dolling describes this residence for us in a letter, September, 1888:

'It contains two very small sitting-rooms, three small bedrooms, and a most miserable kitchen, and none of the rooms are more than seven feet ten inches high. This is not only very inconvenient, but very unwholesome. To-day I am expecting two Oxford men, two Winchester prefects, two boys from London to spend their holidays, and two who have ridden down on tricycles to stay from Saturday to Monday. If you can do a sum, you will guess how many of us will sleep on the floor.'

Inconvenient and unwholesome as this Parsonage was, yet there was a feeling of home about it, and Dolling could say with truth that to many it was a revelation of true brotherhood. 'I can own it is my house,' he wrote, 'that has bound our Winchester boys to the Mission; I am sure that it is my house that has strengthened many in what is called the higher ranks to dare for God in self-sacrifice. I am sure that it is my house that is to our sailors, soldiers, emigrants in the whole world Home. I am sure it is my house that has enabled us to know the real lives of so many of our people, their disposition, their bodily state, and so teaching us in some sense how to deal with them.' But this healing Home life was carried on under conditions that were confessedly alien from common physical healthfulness in the wretched cottage, with its two very small sitting-rooms, and three small bedrooms, and the damp walls and rotten flooring, and after a year of it, Dolling was in very bad health. The doctor insisted on removal and one morning the floor in Dolling's bedroom gave way, and Mrs. Porter, an old lady who helped in the house-work, pushed her leg through into the sitting-room below.

Then it was impossible to delay building a really habitable house, and by 1890 a new Parsonage had been erected on the site of the old cottage, with entrances in Chance Street and Clarence Street. There was real accommodation at last. Dolling had a sitting-room, a waiting-room, and bedroom for himself, and there were four good bedrooms, four cubicles for waifs and strays, a good kitchen, and a large common dining-room thirty feet by fifteen feet. As the number of inmates increased, additional beds were made up in the gallery over the Gymnasium. One rather hideous drawback to the comfort of the house was the fact that, whilst the Gymnasium adjoined it on one side, on the other side stood a bad house that for years defied all Dolling's efforts to get it closed. The shrill and obscene noises from this house sounded plainly in the Parsonage, and, to make matters worse, visitors seeking this place of ill-fame sometimes called at the Parsonage by mistake. Dolling got the house shut up before he left, but its existence was a nightmare for a long time.

Only those who stayed at St. Agatha's Parsonage can know the educational value and the charm of the life within its walls. There were generally fourteen people living in the house, eighteen at dinner every day. And at least forty every Sunday to dinner. The Sunday dinner was a great institution, and there was always enough food to go round, no matter how many extra and unexpected guests arrived. No strict code of rules bound the members of the house or made admission difficult. 'As long as there was enough room we accepted anyone whom it seemed likely we could benefit, always giving preference to those who seemed to need help the most.' No one but Dolling knew the names and circumstances of the men in the house, and often people stayed six months without letting their names or professions be known to the rest. Dolling got over all difficulties of address by giving nicknames to most people. And so thieves and drunkards found themselves in an atmosphere where they were unsuspected, and where some measure of love and respect was meted out to them. Not all the thieves who stayed at St. Agatha's Parsonage became honest men, not all drunkards sober men, but many did. Then there were always the Wykehamists, 'Varsity men, and theological students spending a day or two at the house, and soldiers and sailors always coming and going. Sometimes the young men who came down from Oxford and Cambridge came with great notions of doing good to Landport. Dolling never could stand that. He felt that the open house and its family did not want good being done to it, rather there was good to be got from it; and so the 'superior' young man was sometimes choked off the first day of the visit by Dolling answering his proposals curtly: 'We don't want you to do good; we want to do you good.' 'They want to give lectures, or to teach in night-school or in Sunday-school, or to get up debating societies or cricket clubs, or to boss concerts – in fact, to do anything that means the assertion of their own cleverness or good disposition towards others. How hateful it is! I always kicked at this, sometimes kicked it. I expect these workers do infinitely more harm to themselves than they do good to others.' So Dolling wrote, and so he believed.

St. Agatha's Parsonage was never a 'settlement'; the standpoint of the University settlement, and the tacit assumption of such institutions that the settlement is a place of residence in a strange, uncivilized, unenlightened land were hateful to Dolling. In the last Christmas letter he wrote from Poplar, at the end of 1901, Dolling defends his open house against the suspicion of this standpoint and assumption: 'Somebody said to me the other day, "I suppose you are a kind of settlement?" But that is the last thing we are. We are a family of men and women living in a common home, all helping and being helped by each other, just as we are helping and being helped by the dear people amongst whom we live, not amongst whom we have "settled."' 'Our neighbours' at Landport were 'we,' not 'they,' in the hearts and minds of the dwellers at the Parsonage.

The open house was the place to acquire a knowledge of human nature, a university for all who had the grace to learn its lessons. Even from the men who took advantage of its hospitality and decamped with some other inmate's small possession there was much to be learnt. The sacrament of the common meal was a splendid restorative for tired people, a wholesome corrective of all priggishness. Dolling always encouraged the talking of nonsense as far as possible at meals, and the driving out of dull care by some humorous sally. Children, too, were brought into dinner and tea, for Dolling held that there was no possibility of being really dull in the presence of a little child. 'In my saddest moment,' he once declared, 'when I was feeling sick to death with worry and trouble, wounded oftentimes by my own brethren, the laughter and merriment of a little child would bring us back to ourselves and to God.'

All were welcome, irrespective of creed or denomination, to the common dinner-table, and if the plates ran short, as they did sometimes in the early days, the vegetable dishes would serve. The hot joint, two vegetables, bread and pudding, never failed to provide a meal for all who were present.

If the efforts to reclaim people were not always successful, there was many a man who was restored to health through wholesome food, and Dolling rejoiced when he saw those whose digestions had been ruined by starvation gradually regaining strength, and at last eating a full share. And the social talk at the table did its work. 'If there is any good left in a man, our life, with its freedom, its brotherhood, and its sympathy brings it into play,' Dolling said. 'I can always gauge a man's character by the way he takes our chaff at table. Religion does not spell devotion and worship only, it has a human side, and it is that side I have endeavoured to impress upon my people during the last nine years, and to teach the young men discipline, order and self-respect.

It was a strenuous life for Dolling at St. Agatha's, and the parsonage made great demands upon his health. Every morning at half-past five he would get up to call the boys in the house who were going to work, or the sailors who had to be on board their ships at half-past six. Then he lit the gas-stove in his bedroom, if it was cold, and read or thought out sermons till six. At seven he was in church every morning celebrating the Holy Communion, and at 7.40 he said Morning Prayer. Breakfast was at half-past eight, and after breakfast and all the morning there were letters to be answered, and all sorts of people to be seen. If the study door was open anybody who sought Dolling could be sure of an interview; if it was shut they had to wait till it opened at the exit of the visitor before them. At one o'clock came dinner, and at half-past five tea. In the evening there was a service in church and the clubs or Gymnasium to be visited. At a quarter-past ten came a supper of bread and cheese, and at half-past ten the door to the Parsonage was shut for the night. Anyone who came in after that could only enter by ringing a bell, which brought Dolling himself or one of his helpers down to open the door.

Of course, it took a lot of money to keep this wonderful household going, and the food, though sufficient, was often very scanty. Nothing would have made Dolling give up his open house. In 1887 he writes of the want of food and the value of the house:

'So many people, of course, feeding with us, we have to curtail our manner of food, and we have had to restrict ourselves to meat once a day, and to be content with what our people call "slingers" (bread and butter simple) for other meals. I think it was hard upon us all at first, especially my fellow-workers, but I think we find that it increases the love between us and our people this living in the same way. You will say, "Very unwise, very imprudent"; if so, send my sister, who is our housekeeper, 10s. a week for the purpose, and we will have better food; but the great object is to eat all the same. Nothing seems so churlish as to eat mutton chops and give our guests bread and butter; in that case, the mutton chops could do one no good. Of course, this has made our house expanses heavy – £314 – besides

£100 I pay for my keep (for the year), but we could not do it a penny cheaper, and this open house is the real success of the place; it strikes everyone, and it does so much good to everyone; no one here can put on one side, everyone is on a perfect equality. All over the world at this moment there are my dear boys, who look to this place as their home, from whence all the love they have ever known has reached them. Many a young clergyman looks back to this house as the place where he first learned real heart to heart dealings with men.'

The wholesome, bracing influence of this unique Parsonage was enormous. It made men of thousands who came to it broken in mind or body, and sent them back and out into the world again clothed and whole. Its tone was splendid. 'And as to manners, every single man in my house was a gentleman,' Dolling could boast – 'that is, if thinking for others and treating them with forbearance and tenderness and love, and striving to make them feel at home and at ease, means being a gentleman. The roughest, rudest, most ignorant lad, after a month's residence, had obtained these graces. I have seen deeds of the purest chivalry, self-sacrifice, which the love of God alone can measure; I have seen the withstanding of temptation even to tears and blood; I have seen agonies borne without a word, for fear I should be vexed.'

Of course, it was not always peace and gentleness in the Parsonage. Sometimes things went wrong, boys stole from one another, and men came in drunk. One Sunday at Christmas-time Dolling came in at dinner-time and found 'Blind Willie' – a poor, homeless mudlark, who had lost his sight, and whom St. Agatha's befriended – crying because someone had smashed his hat. The offender refused to confess, and Dolling ordered the dinner to be taken away, and bread and cheese to be the only food eaten till restitution was made. For three days the house stood to bread and cheese rations, and it was always believed that four guests – two clergymen, and a Member of Parliament, and a guardsman, - obtained refreshment elsewhere. It was absolutely necessary that any occasional outbreak of rough horseplay and ill-manners should be checked at once, even by so sharp a lesson as the loss of a hot dinner.

All those years at St. Agatha's Parsonage, Dolling's presence was the centre of the home. Many whom he could not touch by his preaching in church learnt lessons of charity and humility in his house, and recovered self-respect and the consciousness of manhood. His patience and sympathy, and his genial kindliness at the dinner-table were wonderful. No disappointment shook them. But nothing but the presence of a strong, fearless, warm-hearted, earnest, and religious man could have controlled such a household, and guided the destinies of so many of its inmates. Of course, there were helpers – especially Mr. Cornibeer, now a clergyman at Salford, whose influence over the sailor lads was very great – for Dolling needed sympathy and loyalty, and got them. But the Parsonage was Dolling's house, and Dolling's influence was over it all. The family that gathered there are scattered to the far corners of the earth – to mission stations abroad, to country vicarages in England, to newspaper offices in Fleet Street, to snug quarters in Oxford Colleges, to distant naval stations, to soldiers' graves in South Africa, to huts and camps of far-off colonies. But some feeling of fellowship remains, some recognition of the meaning of brotherhood still lurks in Dolling's children, and all who walk this earth of the company who gathered round the hospitable board of St. Agatha's Parsonage take off their hats at the name of Robert Radclyffe Dolling, and salute respectfully the religion he held to. For Dolling's religion was catholic, and at least some aspect of it appealed to every man who stayed at St. Agatha's.

CHAPTER V

DOLLING'S POLITICS

THE son of a North of Ireland Protestant, of a race of Ulster landlords, Dolling was an ardent Radical in politics at the age of twenty-four. Dolling and Stanton of St. Alban's, Holborn, were both strong Disestablishment men and thorough-going democrats in the early Seventies of the Nineteenth Century, and not by any means ashamed, but quite otherwise, of their strong socialistic convictions.

Dolling took to Radicalism as naturally as he took to Church of England Catholicism, and remained till the end the friend and champion of the forlorn and oppressed. Instinctively he was on the side of 'the under dog' in politics, and his impatience of all compromise made him the advocate of radical reforms. Though Dolling became an Imperialist in the last years of his life, and with advancing years he inclined more and more to authority, he never disavowed his Radicalism nor lost his love of liberty.

It was at Portsmouth that Dolling really took an important part in politics.

Portsmouth was represented in Parliament by two Conservatives before 1892, and when, in that year, Messrs. Baker and Clough defeated General Willis and the Hon. Evelyn Ashley, it is not saying too much to say that

Dolling's influence was largely responsible for the Liberal success. He spoke with great effect at all the big meetings, 'proud to recognise in Gladstone a righteous politician,' insisting with passionate eloquence that 'the granting of Home Rule was the only reparation they could make for Ireland's wrongs.' Justice to Ireland and to labour were the notes of his political speeches at that election. He believed in the full and free development of persons and nations, and smote vigorously at all economic and political conditions that hindered such development. Isaac Butt was his 'old friend,' from whom he had learnt that Home Rule was the one thing wanted; under Home Rule Ireland would be free to work out her own salvation. In England there must be a radical change in economic conditions. 'Not money, not pity, not charity could make men free in England,' but only 'the power and opportunity for fair development.'

So Dolling went from platform to platform in Portsmouth in the summer of 1892 to speak for the Liberal candidates, and rejoiced when the declaration of the poll showed that the Conservatives had lost two seats.

Again, at the General Election in 1895, Dolling supported the Liberals and while the Liberal Party throughout the country lost heavily, Portsmouth sent back Messrs. Baker and Clough to the House of Commons with increased majorities. One of the defeated Conservative candidates at that election was Mr. Alfred Harmsworth, in after years one of Dolling's closest friends, and a generous subscriber to the social works at St. Saviour's Poplar.

'The hope for the future of England is the English Democracy,' Dolling declared in those days, and in that hope his political work naturally brought him into contact with Nonconformists of Portsmouth. With them he stood for Church Disestablishment, Home Rule, Temperance Reform, in that spirit – which we call Liberalism – that desires the freedom of the individual from external coercion, and trusts a people to use freedom well.

Of course, a good many people doubted the wisdom of and disapproved such activity in public life, and Dolling, who always liked to make himself understood, delivered a lecture to men in St. Agatha's Church soon after the General Election of 1892, to make his position plain. This lecture he published under the title of 'The Christian Clergyman's Place in Politics,' and as the pamphlet has long been out of print, it may be worth while to give here an extract that contains the substance of his reply to his critics.

'Now, if clergymen have no right whatever to take any part in elections, if it is forbidden to me, because I am a clergyman of the Church of England, to express my political opinions, I am cut off first of all from one of the chiefest of an Englishman's privileges, and, secondly – or I should rather put it firstly – from what I conceive to be the social duty of every Christian man. I feel an interest in politics, and express that interest – first of all because I am Christian, and, secondly, because I am an Englishman. There was a day, you know, when in a large measure the Church of God exercised a mightily influence by speaking the truth upon political subjects. If you take, for instance, the Old Testament, you will find that in the Book of Psalms, which are, I suppose, the part of the Old testament most read by modern Christians, the chief idea which underlies large parts of that wonderful collection is the right of the poor to be heard alike by God and man in all their needs and necessities and to gain the redress of their wrongs. If you go farther into the Old Testament, and take the lives of God's prophets and their words, you will find that as a rule they were essentially political and social reformers, speaking with the authority of the Voice of God, and under the influence of a power which carried them into the palaces of kings, and made their voice heard throughout the land of Israel, and even penetrated into the countries which were brought in contact with their nation. You find these inspired men of God having one single purpose, and that was to preach of the God of Justice, a purpose the execution of which involved a most vigorous onslaught on every kind of oppression and on every species of wrong. In fact, I suppose there has never been gathered together in any volume such magnificent statements of the right of the weak and the helpless as you will find in almost every one of the writings of the Prophets of the Old Testament.

Then you must remember that these are but the forerunners of Jesus Christ, the he is in Himself the gatherer up of all that the Psalmists sung, of all that the Prophets foretold, and therefore you may expect to find in Him also the Champion of the weak and oppressed, and something more than that – the One who preached with a voice which is still sounding throughout all the world, the royalty of every single man, who revealed to man His Divine origin, and showed not merely God's unceasing care for humanity, but God's desire that by his own actions, by using the powers which He had given him, man should be lifted up even to the very highest of all ideals, that there should be no altitude of virtue or intelligence that it should not be possible for man to attain to if he were but true to the power which God had placed in his soul. Looking round on the world, Christ discovered that there were those who had, as it were, absorbed or monopolized these human rights, and rendered well-nigh impossible the development of man, and who had by that very monopoly denied to him the possibility of his attainment to the ideal which God had willed for him. Therefore the voice of Christ, whether it speaks from Galilee, or whether it speaks in the courts of the Temple, sounds and re-sounds to-day, and it shall never cease to re-echo as long as the world has Christianity existing in its midst. It bids a man not merely to be free in the sense in which human laws could give freedom – that is, to be free from the bondage of the oppression with which the cruelty of others had bound him – but to be free in a much higher and truer sense, that he may reach the stature which our Lord Himself foresaw for him when He made him in the Divine image. And if there be in any country in which men live any custom, any privilege of others which denies to men this opportunity, the Christian, be he Priest or be he Layman, must never cease raising his voice until such restriction is removed, until such privilege has been abolished, and the man is able, in the fulness of his manhood, to realize God's eternal will for him.

Therefore I think it is my duty, and I deem it to be the duty of those who think with me, to speak out without bating our breath, and in no temporizing words, in regard to what we believe to be the responsibility that lies upon us as priests and laymen of the Church of England. Because, whether it be true or not, there is an idea – and not merely in town, and in country places – that the Church of England is against the liberties and development of the people of England. Now, mark you, I am not saying it is truly so: it is not for me to judge; but there is not doubt of the fact that it is believed to be so. The recent Welsh elections show this; and I believe in a large measure also, if you were to poll the agricultural districts of England to-morrow on this question, their vote would give the same answer to the inquiry, "Are the clergy of the Church the friends or the enemies of the social and political development of the people of England?"

It is that which makes me feel that we should let men see and know that we, and those who think with us in the Church of England, are determined that it shall be known that we are upon the side of the true development of the English nation, and that we believe honestly that in the carrying out of measures of social amelioration for the future lies the true line for the improvement of the people, and therefore, at all hazards and costs, we are bound to use our influence to see that these measures of reform are passed, and that by men who not merely frame such measures unwillingly, but are in cordial sympathy with that spirit of progress and reform which rouses the social enthusiasm of the great masses of the labouring population. Without a doubt there is a widespread impression among the working classes that the clergy are in league with those who would deprive them of their chance of true development; and therefore we are bound to say that that is untrue, and that there is a large body of the Priesthood of the Church of England – and I believe it to be a much larger body than anyone imagines – who are determined that at all hazards and at all costs they will let the people of England understand that that is a libel upon the Church of England.

'Nay, more than that. If the Church of England is in any sense to be National – and that is what we claim her to be (remember, I am standing now before you as a Priest of the National Church) – she must represent the highest interests of the whole nation. She must not represent one class in the nation; she must not even represent one body of influence in the nation. If she is to claim her share in the great title of Catholic, which means, in one of its senses, Universal, and touching all true human interests, she must recognise the just political aspirations of the people; she must become the National Church in reality, as well as merely in name, not by renouncing any portion of the historic Faith contained in the Creeds of Christendom, but by furthering every true measure for the social uplifting of the whole population of the nation which God has elected her to spiritually represent and minister to. There can now be no doubt that England is rapidly becoming a thoroughly democratic country. I do not appeal solely to elections – whether general or otherwise – in proof of this, but I base this statement upon many larger considerations, patent to every observer of the drift of political opinion among the main body of the people; and therefore, if the Church of England is in any sense to represent the national spirit and the national feeling of England, she must in herself largely be democratic in her sympathies. Of course, she has to represent the other side of English life as well, but if she has a message for the whole of England, she must have that message not for one part, but for the entire nation.'

Dolling's main contention was that as a citizen he was bound to take his part in politics. As a clergyman, he felt he must neither canvas nor employ in any way his church machinery for electioneering ends. Dolling was not in the smallest degree a clericalist. At the altar he could only pray God's will to be done, and in the pulpit exhort obedience to that will. He taught men and women to seek illumination and God's presence in the public worship in church; to tell of the love of God was his business in church. He knew quite well how unfair it would be to make use of his position as parish clergyman, distributing relief and directing many social agencies, to bring any pressure to bear on members of his congregation. His sense of proportion and decency made it impossible for him to elevate devotion to the Liberal Party to the height of obedience to God's laws, and it was God's laws he spoke in church.

The Sunday afternoon lectures to men were a great feature of the work at St. Agatha's. They were attended by men who never came at other times to church, and Dolling at these lectures would deliver his messages on the social and economic ills of the day, speaking with great freedom and strength, dealing with local or national questions without constraint. Yet these addresses were never electioneering speeches; it was the prophet recalling the people of God's eternal laws of justice, and denouncing the oppression of God's people, and not the politician making capital for his party, who delivered them.

And so, though Dolling was a political force in Portsmouth and a strong man on the Radical side, St. Agatha's was never a political church, nor the Winchester

College Mission ever subservient to Liberalism. Men and women of all shades of political opinion knelt at the altars of St. Agatha's and Conservatives, Liberals, and Socialists gathered freely in St. Agatha's Parsonage. No man or woman in the parish feared lest the displeasure of Father Dolling might be incurred by supporting the Conservatives. As a parish clergyman, Dolling knew nothing of the political opinions of his flock. He was sent to minister to them – that sufficed for him. His responsibilities to the town in which he lived drove him to the political platform.

His Radicalism was as thorough in church matters as in national politics. He believed the clergy of the diocese ought to have a voice in the selection of their Bishop, and expressed the desire that his own successor at St. Agatha's might be chosen by the parishioners – by the men and women of the church. As for Disestablishment, the Winchester College Mission was an example of the Voluntary System, and Dolling believed that many of the clergy would be better off if they had to depend on the contributions of their people. From a spiritual point of view, he often declared neither Establishment or Disestablishment would interfere with the Church of God.

Strong democrat as Dolling was at Portsmouth, he was never a mere party man. The democratic idea he believed in and worked for; the machinery of party, the tricks and dodges employed to obtain party success, disgusted him, and kept him out of party organization.

At Poplar there was so much to be done in the parish that Dolling had neither time nor inclination for activity in democratic politics. A great deal of money had to be raised for pressing parochial needs, and to get this money there were sermons to be preached and drawing-room meetings to be addressed in the West End of London. It seemed more important to get money from the rich at the West End for the immediate relief of Poplar than to try and rouse the East-End workmen to demand radical changes in the national economy.

The visit to America produced in Dolling's mind a strong dislike for the professional politician, modified his belief in democracy, and made him look more favourably on a leisured class in the community.

On the question of the South African War Dolling stood with the Government against his Radical and Socialist friends. Yet his deep religious feelings were all against war. Preaching at St. Edmund's, Lombard Street, in Lent, 1894, on 'Soldiers and Sailors,' he foretold the abolition of war by the international union of the labouring people of Europe.

'I must begin by making the awful and solemn declaration that after eighteen centuries of Christianity the object of the "Prince of Peace" had not been attained. War still exists, and therefore it is necessary to speak of soldiers and sailors.

'But the Divine Carpenter will have His revenge, and His revenge will be complete when by means of labour, which He emancipated and glorified, war shall cease throughout the whole world. In a large measure labour is already organized in England, and the workman is learning day by day his own value; but this is at best but a partial step towards peace, and it needs that the English example should be followed upon the Continent, and the movement became cosmopolitan. When once the workman has realised his own powers – powers which, surely, we can teach him can be asserted without anarchy and the disruption of society – when shameful wages and shameful hours and the abominable sweating system, depriving men of the fruits of their labours, shall have ceased universally, as they have begun to cease in England, then the patient pleadings of the Carpenter of Nazareth will be realized, and man – the temporal redeemer of the earth by the sweat of his brow – shall refuse to be manipulated as the enemy of his brethren, either in the sweating dens of financiers, or on the battlefields, or in the armies maintained at present at an impossible cost by politicians or by monarchs for their own selfish purpose.

'The Carpenter will have His revenge, and therefore it is not Utopian to suppose that a day will come when war will cease.'

This feeling remained, and though Dolling supported the War against the Boers, he wrote in March, 1900:

'I wish I could tell you what I think about the War. I am thinking about it all the time, but the thoughts are so deep that they don't come easily to the surface. Every instinct in me rebels against war. It seems to me a contradiction of everything I learned from the lips of Jesus Christ, and of what He intended. I hate, too, so many of the things that seem to have caused it, and yet every day I seem to see more and more how necessary it was – I mean as regards our position in South Africa – and how much more necessary as regards our position at home.'

Dolling accepted the South African War because he believed it 'inevitable.'

'We are not judging those who caused the War,' he said in January, 1900, 'whether English of Boers; both parties thought themselves in the right, and God will judge them. Both nations hereafter will have to take strict account of those who brought affairs to such an *impasse* that war was the only way out of it.'

He held, too, that the War, with its defeats, was a great corrective to national indulgence. And then he had so many friends in the army, officers and men, and his heart went out to these 'children' of his – old Wykehamists, and Portsmouth and East London lads.

Dolling's imperialism came of a deeper sense of authority that was in him. 'Brother Bob' at Mile End and at Portsmouth was a Radical, a thorn in the side of the civil and ecclesiastical powers. Father Dolling, Vicar of St. Saviour's, Poplar, was blessed by Bishops as a beautiful example to other clergymen, and in politics was much less of a rebel and much more of a statesman.

He was drawn to Imperialism, but alive to its dangers, and so he writes in 1901:

'It is hard to maintain Imperialism without a military autocrat....The liberties of England have been won at too great cost for Englishmen ever to surrender them, but it is right for us to remember that they can only be maintained in so far as they are founded upon a higher ideal than mere national success, If we are to be free, indeed, it must be because we have learnt to obey from the highest motive, our duty towards God.

'The autocratic is a far easier method of government, but it keeps its subjects children, and does not make them men.'

Beyond a nominal support of Mr. Sydney Buxton, the Liberal M.P. for Poplar, Dolling took no part in the General Election of 1900. The result of the election he did not believe hopeful for the future, and we find him writing in November, 1900.

'For seven years Lord Salisbury goes back to power with an enormous majority, with a perfectly ineffective opposition, and naturally he will take this as a vote of confidence in himself and in his cabinet. *Naturally*, I say, but not *justly*, because I do not for a moment believe that the majority of the English people willingly endures the abuse in any of our great spending departments, or the way in which they have been managed. The nation felt that it could not give the African settlement into the hands of Sir Henry Campbell-Bannerman and Sir William Harcourt, and therefore it was compelled to leave the settlement in the hands of the Government; but to imagine that the nation approves of the way in which the Admiralty, the War Office, and the Board of Trade are managed, or that it has any confidence in the heads of those departments, I do not for a moment believe. Lord Salisbury is wonderfully generous to those who work with him. He knows, I take it, very little about the mind of England except on the one point of the War; he has a dislike to trusting young men. All that is easy to be understood of a man of his age, but I do not think that it is hopeful for the future. And then the ever-shadowing presence of Mr. Chamberlain, actually everywhere, his ability as a fighter, his thick-skinned nature, which enables him to wound deeply the friend of yesterday, makes him more than a master mind in the present Cabinet. All this seems fraught with danger, and all that we can do is to pray, and to believe as we pray, that God can and will overrule it all for the best.'

At Poplar Dolling had lost his faith in the Liberal Party, and was without confidence in the Conservatives.

In municipal matters he remained entirely Progressive. Nothing shook his conviction that land monopoly was unjust and evil in its results.

The thing to be noted is that Dolling, with all his strong political convictions, was never a political clergyman. He never went about the country speaking on political and social questions. He could not believe that in becoming a priest he had got rid of his responsibilities as a man and a citizen. He held that it was his right and his duty to take his share in the politics of his age, to utter his opinions freely on all questions of the day. The first and chief business of Dolling's mind and heart was to minister to people. This ministry he believed he fulfilled in church – at the altar, in the pulpit, and in the confessional – on the political platform at public meetings, and by the provision of food, fresh air, health, and joy to those who lacked these things; and in that faith he lived and died.

CHAPTER VI

DOLLING'S ATTITUDE TO THE LABOUR MOVEMENT

The Labour Movement – the movement expressed in the agitations of Socialists and trade unionists – aims at securing a fuller life for the wage-earners of the country. It seeks to shorten the hours of labour, to raise wages, to obtain provision for old age, to abolish slums, and to place the opportunity of work before every man. To many it stands for more than this, for a 'Co-operative Commonwealth,' wherein all shall labour for the good of the community, and where the present glaring inequalities of riches and poverty shall be no more.

There have always been men filled with this ideal of a reign of social righteousness, and it was natural that Dolling should have supported the Labour Movement.

Two things drew him to it. His intense sympathy for the down-trodden, the labouring and heavy-laden, and his passion for justice.

Around him at Mile End Road, at Portsmouth, and at Poplar, were thousands of people wanting food, clothes, fresh air, better houses, whose lives were impoverished and crippled for lack of these things. Many of these people worked hard, lived temperately and honestly, and yet were in distress. Some sought anxiously for work and could not find it. Love moved Robert Dolling to seek to supply their needs, justice impelled him to denounce the conditions of society that kept multitudes in misery.

'Justice first, Charity afterwards,' is the title of Robert Dolling's sermon for the Christian Social Union at All Saints', Notting Hill, Lent, 1894. It is quite worth while to look into this sermon for it contains the refusal to accept pauperism as a wholesome thing in a Christian society, and deprecates the exaltation of almsgiving into the chief Christian virtue.

'That very charity which should make men strong in the very truest meaning of the word strength is by universal consent translated by the fatal word almsgiving – a virtue, if it be a virtue at all, full of danger both to him who gives and him who receives. To the vast majority of men giving is a real pleasure, especially when it doesn't cost them anything in personal comfort. May I illustrate this. We are told by Bishops and by others that they must have large incomes. Twenty-five years ago it would have been said – to spend on themselves. Now it is said – to support the different charities in their dioceses. Can any position be more full of danger? If these sums are really wanted for Diocesan charities, and the Bishop does not desire the pleasures of patronage, let them be administered by a Diocesan Board. And surely the same argument applies to the vast incomes inherited by men at no personal labour, and to the enormous sums accumulated by men in trade. If this almsgiving is to be anything better than a mere subtle form of self-indulgence, above all let us preach that God is only dishonoured by gifts that cost the giver nothing.'

The preacher finds excuse for the prominence given to almsgiving in the earlier days of the Church. To have proclaimed a fully-developed Christian civilization under the Roman Empire was impossible.

'What the Church did at the time, and probably it was all that she could do, was first to secure her own existence by refusing to dissolve at the bidding of the civil power, and by propagating herself as an organized society; and secondly, not to attempt to remove such evils as slavery all at once, but to mitigate them by urging on her members their duty of almsgiving in the widest sense. Thus she fed and clothed Lazarus rather than endeavoured to overcome the cause which created on one side Lazarus, on the other side Dives. Surely *our* duty is to face the problem and to discover the cause.'

Then comes insistence on the point that the only Christlike rule in business is, 'Do I do justly?' not 'Do I make money?'

'The man, for instance, who out of the labour of a number of boys and girls makes his fortune without considering the hours they work, the surroundings they work in, whether it is possible for them to develop physically, intellectually, spiritually – surely he must answer for the failure of true development in each one of these. This man who, because labour is disorganized, or because there are so many unemployed, can induce men to work for less money than they can possibly live on is surely not only responsible for the deterioration of the man, but for the suffering of the man's wife and family, and becomes in some way the cause of why the children of the man he employs grow into the wretched class of loafers and of vagabonds, simply because neither brain nor body is nourished by proper food.'

The moral of the sermon is that poverty comes of injustice and cannot be cured by charity.

'A very large percentage of those in the workhouse have by their sweat and blood created the fortunes of the rich. It is the sheerest folly to say they are all in there because they are loafers or drunkards, and even the loafer and drunkard are society-created. Some, no doubt, are born so, as others are born lunatics, but they ought to be protected against themselves and gently treated; but the majority are so because they have never had a chance. I should not believe that God was just if the majority were born to be drunkards, born to be loafers. But, at any rate, if we cannot save them now, let England see to it that she ceases to create such a class in future. There are houses enough, food enough, teaching enough, work enough and love enough in this world of injustice for all God's children. Let the Church teach some doctrine a little more drastic than almsgiving, a little more according to the doctrine of Christ, than, when you have made your pile, live in purple and fine linen yourself, provide all luxuries for your children, take a sitting in the fashionable church, and give £20 a year for charity, and thus create and insurance against the fire in which every man's work is tried.... We want to enlarge our ideal of the word "immoral." Why should we restrict it to only one kind of sin? Paul condemns fornication and uncleanness, but he condemns also "covetousness, which is idolatry." Let us use the same words – nay, rather let us see how covetousness, beyond all other sins, creates in other men the very sins we call immoral, because it deprives men of all true chances.'

Here then, is the explanation of Dolling's sympathy with Socialism and the Labour Movement. He believed they made for that justice which would remove the burden of privation and misery from the back of the working folk. If in later days Dolling took a smaller part in labour politics, it was not that he desired justice less, but that his love for the people would not brook delay. He saw the ills that could be redressed immediately by money, and his active soul could not wait for economic changes in the State. He hastened to do all the good that could be accomplished in his day and generation, and left the radical changes to be effected by others.

At Portsmouth, especially in the early years of his charge of the Winchester College Mission, Dolling took a prominent position in all local labour movements.

In that terrible winter of 1894 he threw open his schoolroom for the meetings of the Unemployed, and on the Board of Guardians and on public platforms pleaded their cause.

At trade unionist meetings and trades council demonstrations in Portsmouth Dolling was a regular and a very popular speaker. On such occasions he urged the trade unions to take political action and secure the election of labour Members in Parliament and the Town Council; or he would dwell on the unselfishness of the trade unionist agitation, which called upon workmen to practise personal self-denial for the sake of others, and which had won better conditions in the matter of hours and wages by the self-sacrifice of the men who had gone before.

When the Typographical Association established a branch in Portsmouth, Dolling was there to give the compositors his benediction, and for years he helped in the difficult work of trying to organize that somewhat flabby body of people the shop-assistants. In this battle for the shop-assistants, and in the battles for temperance and social purity, Dolling found a stanch ally in the Rev. C. Joseph, the minister of Lake Road Baptist Chapel. Once when Father Dolling was sitting in St. Agatha's hearing confessions a messenger came rushing into the church to ask him to come to a meeting of shop-assistants in Mr. Joseph's chapel. 'Please come,' said the messenger, 'or we shall lose the day.' Dolling had his surplice off at once, and strode along to Lake Road. It was as natural for him to plead for justice in a Baptist Chapel as in any other place, and his appearance in his cassock and biretta struck no one as incongruous. When he had made his speech he want back again to his church.

Dolling's support of trade unions did not prevent him from seeing possible dangers in their success. He held that everything that tended to make the workman more intelligent, and more self-reliant was 'a tremendous gain,' and that the better hours and better wages won by trade union effort had this tendency. Of the dangers he wrote in 1896:

'Of course there are two dangers: first, as the Unions grew stronger, they had a tendency to look at all questions merely from the workman's point of view; and, secondly, there was a danger of the individual wasting his increased wages and leisure in bad ways. In all acts of emancipation the first enjoyment of liberty may turn to license, but such license never lasts very long; and I think, looking back over the last thirty years' history of the Labour Movement in England, one might say that this license has almost never existed. At any rate, I was continually struck with the enthusiasm for righteousness that I discovered amongst the majority of the leading men with whom I was brought in contact.'

Dolling expressed his opinion of the leaders in the Labour Movement in the following words:

'For all those who are interested in the Labour Question there can be no thought so full of thankfulness to God and of hope for the future as the knowledge that the vast majority of labour leaders are deeply religious men.'

Trusting the people as he did, and with this confidence in the accredited working-class leaders, Dolling, of course, favoured the return of Labour candidates to the House of Commons. But he pointed out that Labour members ought not to be the paid delegates of particular trade unions, but that their salaries should come from the nation, otherwise they would feel bound to the interests of the people who paid them; and it those interests clashed with the interests of the community, they would vote against the welfare of the latter for the sake of their particular trade unions. This advice might well be pondered just now, when many trade unions are arranging to get special and sectional representation in the House of Commons.

The Old Sunday Afternoon Lectures to men at St. Agatha's were often full of the spirit of socialism. 'The land of every country belonged to the people of that country,' Dolling would declare; and he spoke with regret of the fact that in England 'a few men had all the land and another small class all the capital.'

In an address on 'The Living Wage' in 1894, he pointed out the vast fortunes acquired by business men, and asked the question, 'Could these fortunes be amassed if those who had created the property were paid a living wage?' And then came the answer, delivered with Dolling's characteristic earnestness, ' No – emphatically no!'

In the same address there is a sharp reference to 'the modern pretending Christian,' who shifted his responsibility to his neighbour on to the State or some philanthropic committee. 'Doubtless the reply of these to the reproach of Jesus Christ, "When I was naked ye clothed Me not, sick and in prison ye visited Me not," would be: "Oh, though we neglected you when you were naked and unclothed, we knew there was Board of Guardians; when we saw you sick and visited you not, we knew there was a pauper doctor who would attend you; and when you were hungry and we failed to relieve you, we knew there were charity agencies that would give you a ticket for groceries."'

At the Debating Society he established in Portsmouth for the fuller discussion of these questions Dolling would speak with equal frankness.

With good cause the members of the Portsmouth Radical Club declared on his death their 'admiration and appreciation of the Rev. R. R. Dolling's efforts to lighten the distress of the many with whom he associated during his residence in Portsmouth,' and their 'recognition of the valuable services rendered by him to all the advanced movements, and of the unflinching manner that he displayed when dealing with unpopular causes.'

At Poplar there was less political and Socialist work, but the question of overcrowding was ever present in St. Saviour's Parish. In a long article on 'Overcrowding' in the *Parish Magazine*, December, 1899, Dolling maintains that the Housing Problem is but part of the larger Social problem, and that its solution depends upon our settlement of the Land Question. He writes of the opening up of new districts in the suburbs as follows:

'There are two difficulties to be met and faced. First, there is the compulsory purchase of the land at its present value without the unearned increment which the approach of population always creates. That, of course, has been the initial wrong; the value of land sometimes multiplied itself many hundredfold without a penny being spent upon it, and all that profit has gone to the owner. Unless, therefore, the present letting value is taken as the basis of compulsory sale, any large creation of cheap houses would be impossible.' The second difficulty was the absence of a cheap and constant railway service.

The article concludes with an appeal to justice and conscience, and it is Dolling, the Christian agitator, who speaks:

'There is, therefore, I take it, only one remedy which really cuts at the root of the evil – the attacking of those two great monopolies, the land and the railway system, which, united together, prevent any extension of houses which can be of any benefit to the really respectable poor; and yet even when these have been, as they must be, battled with the vanquished, you will still have the slum-dweller creating his slum. But when statesmen have spoken their last work, the Christian has still a word to speak. Create within the respectable poor the longing for all these things; stir the soul till it is utterly discontented with and abhors its present surroundings; make the father and mother realize that all duty to their children is impossible as things are.... It is almost impossible to get true statistics of overcrowding for fear anybody should be dispossessed. The truth is we have not got the vigour of body or the keenness of mind to care about these things. We have always lived in them; we feel we cannot alter them. And nothing but Christian enthusiasm can alter them – aye, and Christian enthusiasm could alter even the loafer and his slum. And so, while we must do our best to insist upon present legislation being put into force and future legislation being created, Christianity must labour on in making the heart and conscience of the man right, and then he will insist upon an environment which will be possible for himself and his fellows.'

Those words represent the sum of all Dolling's teaching on industrial questions. Let the State do justice, all of us as citizens doing our part, and let the Christ so inform our lives that we cannot rest till evil has been rooted out.

The Poplar Labour League – a Socialistic workmen's organization for securing labour representation has always been friendly with the local clergy (it has had for its Treasurer the Rev. H. A. Kennedy and the Rev. C. Chandler, Rector of Poplar), and, of course, Dolling supported it. Mr, Will Crooks, the Labour member for Poplar on the London County Council, and the present Mayor of Poplar, lives in Northumberland Street just by St. Saviour's, and a strong affection existed between the Vicar of St. Saviour's and the genial labour agitator, who has devoted his life to his neighbours in Poplar.

Often when Father Dolling passed by Mr. Crooks' house on his way to the City he would drop in for a hasty consultation on some local question or to borrow a Blue-Book or report. And when the representative of the Poplar Labour League was made Mayor of Poplar in 1901, the Vicar of St. Saviour's expressed his pleasure.

'I am rejoiced to find my dear friend, Will Crooks, the Mayor of Poplar. I have not seen him yet with his gold chain and red robes, though I half think he ought to come to our Social on December 3 thus dressed; notwithstanding that I like to see him best in his shirt-sleeves and carpet slippers, having just jumped up from his breakfast to give advice, counsel, comfort, or help to some poor soul standing at his door. No one knows as he does the needs of Poplar. No one has greater tact in representing these needs, greater courage in demanding that they shall be satisfied.... In this great constituency all respect him, and many bless him for acts of kindness and help of which the world knows nothing.'

This tribute is not a Churchman, for Mr. Will Crooks has never been attached to a Church, but to an East-End workman. It was enough for Dolling that Will Crooks was a man, doing a man's work, when so many were shirking their part. He loved to see men battling for justice, and whenever he found them his heart went out to them.

The weakness, the factions, the jealousies in the Labour Movement were intolerable to Robert Dolling, but he rejoiced in its courage. For the weakness of the humble his compassion was unbounded; but for the weakness of men in responsible positions, the failure that accompanied pretentious claims, he had no pity, but scorn.

CHAPTER VII

DOLLING'S TREATMENT OF SOCIAL QUESTIONS.

Dolling's sympathy with the Labour Movement, his advocacy of political reform, and his active interest in the solution of social questions, all sprang from one source, the thirst for justice and the love of his kind, and were directed to one end, the fuller development of man. Life, and life more abundantly, he desired for the people whom he saw stunted and starved around him. So on all such questions as national education, the administration of the Poor Law, temperance, the treatment of our soldiers and sailors, and the public water-supply – all matters affecting directly the welfare of his parishioners – Dolling had something to say, some message to deliver, and some part to play in seeking a solution.

For three years (1892-95) he sat on the Portsmouth School Board, chosen by the people as a Progressive, and determined to make the common schools of the town as efficient as possible. The Portsmouth School Board in those days had to spend heavily in providing accommodation for the growing population, and its teachers were in many cases underpaid, and the classes in the school far too large. Against both these evils Dolling spoke strongly, but he recognised that the ratepayers were chiefly responsible for the small salaries and under-staffing, and always expressed appreciation of the work of the Board. It was impossible to measure what England owed to the Board Schools, he would say, and of their benefits to education in Portsmouth he spoke with equal emphasis. At the same time, he believed strongly in his Church Schools, both at Landport and Poplar, rebuilding them and taking every pains to bring them up to the standard of the Board School. Why, it is sometimes asked, should Dolling, and men like him who believe in School Boards, bother about Church Schools of their own? The answer is that Dolling wanted a closer and more personal touch with the children than the Board School afforded, and a fuller and more definite religious instruction. He held that it was not the business of the State to teach religion; that an unsectarian religion was impossible, because every teacher must have a bias; and that the right thing would be for each denomination to appoint teachers to give the religious instruction in the schools. The difficulty in the way of this, he declared, was 'the laziness and jealousy of those who ought to be the religious teachers.' The ordinary Bible lessons of the Board School and of many voluntary schools seemed to Dolling quite inadequate. There was far too much of the Old Testament in there lessons he contended, and not enough of 'those saving truths which even quite young children can apprehend and assimilate to themselves.' In his Church Schools he found a more humane atmosphere than in the Board Schools, and the closer touch they afforded made it less difficult to find work for the children when they left school. That a School Board, like any other public elected body, was apt to become merely mechanical in its methods, Dolling saw with misgivings, for he knew that in such a case the teachers became mechanical too. Let the education be thorough, let there be a personal bond between teachers and scholars, and let the appointed religious teachers do their duty in the schools, was Dolling's attitude to elementary education. He had no sympathy for Church Schools that were under-staffed, and inferior and unsanitary buildings were not to be tolerated. 'There is no scandal so injurious to the Church of England as a school that is not wholesome or properly staffed,' he once wrote in an article in the *Pilot*. Education in his mind was an environment of childhood second only in importance to the home, and it was by a better environment that he looked for the prevention of weakly and vicious characters, and the building up of strong and healthy men and women.

On the Portsmouth Board of Guardians Dolling laboured for years in this spirit for the children of the Poor Law. He tried to get the schools for these children away from the Workhouse buildings, and, though defeated in this, managed to effect reforms that included the provision of pocket-handkerchiefs and the better treatment of the sick. What struck Dolling on the Board of Guardians was that the expenses of management and the creation of plant were altogether out of proportion to the amount expended on the actual relief of the poor – the definite object of the Board. He found too, that Guardians were often recklessly extravagant in all the outward part of their organization, the part seen by the public, and shockingly mean in matters of small expenditure which only affected the comfort and well-being of the Workhouse inmates. Dolling was never content with the moving of a resolution, the mere expression of opinion. The recording of a minute in favour of some reform is a very different thing from the reform itself. In many unsatisfactory details of Workhouse management Dolling had to adopt unusual methods before his colleagues on the Board of Guardians could be moved to improve matters. Once he found the children at tea, and taking this liquid in the same mugs that had done duty at dinner-time for soup-plates. Grease and fat floated on the top of the tea, and when Dolling expressed surprise and disgust, the attendant assured him that the mugs were never washed after dinner. At the Board meeting Dolling complained indignantly of this neglect, but the Board refused to order any washing-up after dinner. 'The children don't mind, and we must not be too particular,' was the answer. At the next meeting of the Board Dolling arranged for a child's mug with the tea and fat to be placed before each member, the Board was taken by surprise; it had to confess the liquid looked loathsome, and from that day the children had clean mugs for tea. It was only a comparatively small matter, perhaps, but the incident shows Dolling's characteristic way of getting a thing through.

Temperance and social purity are very closely related. In Portsmouth, as in all naval and military towns, the inducements to intemperance and impurity were enormous. St. Agatha's district, when Dolling came down in 1885, contained a population of nearly 6,000, living in 1,100 houses and fifty-two of these were public-houses and fifty were of ill-fame. The temperance work was not a mere total abstinence agitation, it was a serious effort to grapple with the abuses of the drink traffic. The enormous number of public-houses in Portsmouth and the purposes for which these houses were used were the two points Dolling chiefly laboured at. The houses were tied houses, and the drink trade was in the hands of a small number of brewers. The publican was obliged to sell a certain quantity of liquor or leave. To effect the required sale of liquor, the publican, Dolling pointed out, had to resort to all sorts of objectionable practices. 'Everyone knows that there are innumerable ways of adulterating or faking-up drink; that, if gambling and betting are allowed, men will congregate; that, if bad characters fill the bar, certain men will stay there; that, if the singing of vulgar songs is allowed, it is a great attraction and makes men who roar the choruses all the more thirsty.'

That many publicans were too high-minded to employ these methods Dolling admitted thankfully, but the fear of starvation compelled others.

A large reduction in the number of licenses, the abolition of back and side entrances to public-houses, because they gave great facilities to illicit drinking, and the prevention of loitering for immoral purposes in public-houses, were the principal items of the temperance programme, and a Vigilance Committee of which Canon Jacob (now Bishop of Newcastle) was chairman, and the Rev. C. Joseph hon. Secretary, was formed in Portsmouth to get these reforms carried out. Through the energies of Dolling and other members of this Committee, the Watch Committee of the Town Council was stirred up to suppress certain outward signs of evil, and the public-houses largely ceased to be the open resort of prostitutes. But the excessive number of licensed houses remained untouched.

Dolling never looked to Parliament for Temperance Reform. I don't think he ever believed in Local Veto or municipalization. He never had any real liking for protective legislation, even when he realized the necessity of it. That man, by the development of character and force of religion, should become temperate; that brewers and publicans should ply their trade with strict honesty, and refuse to make drunkards; and that local authorities should see that the public-houses were decent and clean and not more in number than other shops, was what he desired.

If the public-houses could not be closed, Dolling did succeed in getting the disorderly houses of vice excluded from his parish, and of the fifty that stood in 1885, only three remained ten years later. His method was to write to the landlord, explaining the uses to which the house was put, and calling upon him to take only respectable tenants. If the landlord declined to take any notice, Dolling would speak about it, and mention the name of the landlord publicly, and shame him into better ways. But very often the landlord was quite willing to get rid of unsatisfactory tenants directly his attention was called to the matter. That respectable people should make profits by the ownership of brothels was infamous to the Missioner of St. Agatha's; but for the women who plied their unfortunate trade he had nothing but compassion.

One of Dolling's sermons on the treatment of soldiers and sailors, preached in London for the Christian Social Union, Lent, 1894, provoked great excitement in

Portsmouth. In this sermon allusion was made to the terrible temptations of drink and impurity to which the soldiers and sailors were exposed in garrison towns and seaports, and the preacher described these towns as 'sinks of iniquity.' The Mayor of Portsmouth and the brewers and their friends immediately lashed themselves into a fury of indignation, and the Mayor, accompanied by two police officers, made a tour of inspection of the public-houses the following night. Inasmuch as the Mayor declared that he had visited fifty public-houses and beer-shops in the worst part of the borough between 9.40 and 11 p.m. without seeing any drunkenness, it was generally felt in the town that, anyhow, the number of public-houses must be excessive, and that to visit fifty houses in eighty minutes hardly left time to investigate the conditions within. A town's meeting of protest against the sermon was threatened, but a little consideration convinced Portsmouth that the preacher's facts were only too true, and that it was selfish fear lest visitors should be kept away from Southsea that had prompted the agitation against the sermon. So the storm blew over, and Dolling wrote of it two years later: 'I believe myself that the row did the town a great deal of good, and I am thankful to think that when I left it I received from all kinds and sorts of people the most appreciative letters, one of the very kindest being from one of the largest brewers.'

In this same sermon Dolling took up the wrongs of the soldier and sailor in the hands of the Government, and enumerated certain pressing needs. Until the nations abandoned war, it was monstrous that we should treat our soldiers and sailors unfairly, he declared. 'A man is drawn into the ranks of the army on practically false – I say shamefully false – pretence. Nominally he receives a shilling a day and rations. What are the facts? Threepence out of every shilling is stopped to supply extra food necessary for his bodily health, whether he will or no.

'A halfpenny is compulsorily stopped for washing; thus his shilling becomes eightpence-halfpenny. But these deductions do not stop here: barrack damages, library, hair-cutting, and oftentimes other compulsory subscriptions make a still further reduction, so that at the end of the week the shilling is seldom more than sevenpence.'

The soldier was also imposed upon by the promise of a free kit.

'This kit is by Government renewed from time to time, but his under kit consisting of three pairs of socks, two shirts, two towels one little bit of soap, and other things necessary for what is called cleaning, he has to maintain for seven long years. He has to show his kit monthly, and if he is lacking, he has to pay for new ones, and he is punished as well.'

The pay in the navy is a little in advance of that in the army, but the sailor has to buy and keep up all his kit.

It was not merely the question of pay that called for an answer; the treatment of the sailor's wife and family demanded attention, and it is still necessary to repeat the complaints voiced by Dolling in 1894.

'The sailors carry their lives in their hands for your sakes. It is a noble thing, truly, to die for one's country, but if you leave wife and children behind to beggary, and worse, surely the country does not fulfil her part of the bargain. I need not refer to the shameful management of the Patriotic and *Victoria* Funds; but shameful as is the provision made for widows and orphans in the *Victoria* case, happy, you may say, is the woman whose husband happens to die in a crowd. If he had fallen overboard on some stormy night, or been killed pursuing a slaver on the African coast, his wife and children would have got nothing at all.'

Fair wages, some provision for the wife and child of the man who has died on duty, opportunity for marriage, and the removal of the overwhelming temptations to drunkenness and impurity in our naval and military towns – these were the things Dolling's soldier and sailor friends stood most in need of. It was not mainly for the sake of the army or the navy he pleaded, but for the sake of the men in the service – his friends – whom he saw robbed and wounded by official injustice daily, and left to perish by the roadside, uncared for by the Church.

Soldiers and sailors are not much in evidence at Poplar, and the seafaring men of merchant ships stick mostly to the East India Dock Road. But East London had its own social question in 1898 – the question of an adequate supply of water.

Dolling came to St. Saviour's, Poplar, in July, and in August the whole district was suffering from Water Famine. The East London Waterworks Company has a monopoly, and it has failed on more than one occasion to maintain its supply in dry seasons. At the end of August, 1898, each householder was restricted to a daily supply of six hours – the rest of the day no water was forthcoming. Only a very few houses had cisterns or any means of storage, and the result of the famine was misery and sickness; for the days and nights of that September were very hot. In St. Saviour's Vicarage and the parish schools there was the same lack of water that was troubling the whole parish. The Vicar wrote to the *Times*, he expressed himself forcibly to several newspaper interviewers, he obtained stoppered jars for storing drinking-water for more than 600 houses, and he addressed a big open-air meeting at the Dock Gates. But he did more than this. With his churchwardens he summoned a public meeting to be held in the church, and presided over a gathering of some 500 men. The local County Councillors, Messrs. McDougall and Crooks, Mr. J. F. King, the Chairman of the Sanitary Committee of the Poplar Board of Works, and Mr. Matley, the headmaster of St. Saviour's Day-schools, all took part in the proceedings, and the result of the meeting was a resolution 'strongly protesting against the repeated failures of the East London Waterworks Company to maintain a constant water-supply, and expressing the belief that no effective remedy will be found until the water-supply of London is placed under public control.'

It was quite an unusual and unconventional thing to hold such a meeting in a church, but it seemed quite natural to Dolling, in whose eyes there never was a hard-and-fast line between things secular and religious. 'It is very fit,' he said, 'that we should meet in our Father's house to try and find some way to amend the awful state of things brought about by the insufficient water-supply. There is no other room in the parish big enough for the purpose, and therefore the church is the only place.'

In the parish magazine Dolling stated the case against 'this monstrous water company,' as he called it:

'The East London Water Company divides a dividend of 7 per cent., oftentimes more. We are bound to pay our rates, whether we get the water or not. In the very worst time of year, at a time when diphtheria and scarlet fever always increase among us, at a time when we are sweltering in heat, and when little children are at death's door continually, they restrict us to six hours a day, and that not regularly supplied. Our good churchwardens feel with me that it is our duty to invite all male parishioners to express their opinion on this point, and I thank God that it is in His house that we are going to meet, and I hope we shall not cease our agitation until this Company is dispossessed of its powers, and they are placed under public control.'

Yet, when the famine was over, the interest in the question of the Company's monopoly melted away, and four years hence East London is still as far from the public control of its water as ever.

Of course, some people, who did not live in East London, were shocked at the meeting, and it was even said that 'Dolling has got up this water famine to gain notoriety.'

Dolling did all that seemed possible to ease the distress, to call attention to the injury, and to rouse a public opinion that would destroy the cause of the wrong. He believed that the Company had failed to fulfil the conditions under which they held the monopoly, and that the only thing to be done was to take the water-supply out of the Company's hands. And in this, as in all other matters of social importance, he held it his duty as a citizen, and as a parish clergyman, to take a strong line. It was impossible for him to look upon suffering – especially suffering caused by the ignorance and selfishness of those in authority – and remain silent. As he pleaded to God for his people, so with pen and speech he pleaded for his people in press and pulpit.

CHAPTER VIII

DOLLING'S LOVE FOR THE OUTCAST AND HOMELESS

In Dolling was that rare combination, the priest and the good Samaritan. He was always the priest pleading to God for his people, the good shepherd ministering to his flock, and the Samaritan tending and rescuing all the wounded and afflicted whom he chanced to meet upon the road. And it was not at all because he was an ordained clergyman of the Church of England that he did these things, but because he was just Dolling – a man who felt for and understood the infirmities of his fellows. There was no change in his character or in his way of life when he was ordained. Robert Dolling's heart always went out to the cry of human distress, every outcast and forlorn person claimed his sympathy. The thief who had placed himself outside the recognition of society, and who divided his time between the streets and the gaol; the man who had gone under in the stress of the struggle for existence; the clergyman who had fallen from his position through drink; the outcast woman of the streets; the homeless soldier and sailor; the child who had never known the love of parents; the tramp and the loafer – all had a place in Dolling's heart. He learnt to love the boys who stole things in the old days of Father Stanton at St. Alban's.

'We never call them thieves,' Mr. Stanton said to me when I asked him about the period of Dolling's life. 'Of course, they take things sometimes and go to gaol, but we never call them thieves. They are our boys, you know, and I've always had a class of thirty or forty of them. We never speak of them as thieves.'

So it was with Dolling. They stole things sometimes, but they were his boys still; and he couldn't think of them as thieves, but as his children, whose failings were not to be trumpeted abroad, lest shame should fall on the family of which he had made them members. He held, too, that the best cure for dishonesty is the planting of self-respect; to trust a man, to make him feel that, though he has stolen, and been convicted and punished, you still believe in him, is the first step towards making an honest man of him. Dolling never accepted the ordinary failings in dishonesty and intemperance as normal states. There might be exceptional cases in which kleptomania and dypsomania were diseases, and could only be treated as such; the average men who stole and got drunk did so from accidental causes, and under different and more kindly circumstances, would be honest and sober. Experience and charity taught him to believe in man, to appeal to the nobler and not the baser instincts of his children, and taught him that what we expect to find in others we very often do find. He looked for honesty and purity and temperance in all men, and searched for these qualities, till the thief admitted there was honesty within him which could be utilized, and the impure and intemperate confessed their preference for a cleaner life. Sin was abnormal in Dolling's eyes; to love God and keep His commandments was the appointed life for man.

Of course, the men who stole things did not always give up their habits even when they came to live with Dolling. One lad, who lived with him at Portsmouth, and who came under the influence of religion and was confirmed, fell away after spending nine months at the Parsonage. Dolling so trusted this lad that he gave him his letters to take to the post, and even his money to take to the bank; and then one day, on the eve of a big race meeting he stole a letter of Dolling's, which he knew contained a postal order for a pound. But that is not the end of the story – which is told in full, with many others, in the 'Ten Years in a Portsmouth Slum.'

The lad went to America, but he turned up again at St. Agatha's, having worked his passage back in a cattle-ship. 'He came just to stay two days with me,' Dolling wrote, 'to tell me his failures and successes. When last I heard from him he had been going on all right since his return.'

And Dolling comments on this: 'How magnificent are these efforts to do right, in spite of over whelming temptation! How infinitely more heroic than our snug contentment at our own honesty, who have never had cause to steal. And yet, falling, in a moment, discovery, gaol, despair. Has Christian society not better method?'

Sometimes Dolling found it necessary to adopt severer measures, and one man who had become a thief, and who walked all the way down to Landport to implore Dolling's protection, was not taken into the house. Dolling saw that the repentance was unreal, and that, had he been saved from the legal penalty that was threatening his liberty, he would merely have stolen again at the next temptation, and so he told him he must give himself up and go to gaol. The man thought it hard, but submitted. And then one day, just before Dolling left St. Agatha's, the thief was released, and came straight down to Portsmouth, to be received with open arms. 'The Discipline of gaol gave him the grace of amendment,' Dolling wrote. 'Our help restored to him faith in himself, and there is no doubt that he will do well.' Dolling took him up to London with him, and then sent him to America, where the man had friends who would help him.

The men who had fallen through drink, whom Dolling sheltered, were mostly clergyman, and they were more difficult to help than the lads who stole. When there was a real desire to be healed, residence in Dolling's house effected a cure sooner or later; but when the will had gone, and it was merely shelter that the inebriate wanted, the case was hopeless. It seemed very sad to turn such men out, and Dolling always thought it hard that no sort of home was provided by the Church of England for its fallen ministers. The workhouse and the gaol were the last places on earth where broken-down clergymen could regain hope. But there was no room in the Parsonage at Landport or at Poplar for people who had lost the desire for better things, and the drunkard who loved drink more than life had to go. As long as there was any vestige of will, as long as there was any spark that could be kindled into a fire of purpose for good, Dolling tended the outcast, no matter how great had been the fall. But when neither will nor desire would respond the man had to leave, to sink into a lower hell, in which perchance, touching the nethermost bottom of human misery, he might in the hour of crucifixion find the light which would yet lead him to Paradise.

For the last eight years at Landport there were always one or two inebriates in the Parsonage. They did not dress as clergymen, nor were their circumstances known to the rest of the house. Besides, there were always people coming and going, and curiosity was never tolerated. Everyone in the house came to see Dolling; his affairs were known to 'the Father' – that was enough.

Dolling's tenderness and tact in dealing with fallen clergymen were wonderful. He always made so much allowance for them. 'It is so hard for them to live like gentlemen,' he said, 'when very often they have not got enough income to keep body and soul together.' Then he understood the loneliness of many a curate's life, 'especially if he is a little on in years, so that the female part of the congregation do not admire him.' The discomfort of lodgings, the want of proper food, the absence of congenial society, and the fact of having to preach when there was little vital force, all these things Dolling knew encouraged the fatal habit of drinking in many a curate. Living with him they caught something of his devotion, something of his faith, and as the days went by their religious feelings were quickened, and they understood that if they had fallen and degraded their office, they had not sinned beyond redemption. There came a day when they longed to renew their work, and to help others to escape from the pit into which they had sunk. With great care Dolling would seek out curacies for them, and they would leave his house clothed once more in the priest's dress and in their right minds.

The Church authorities came to recognise in Dolling a man who could cure difficult cases of clerical failure, and Bishops and Archdeacons would ask him to take charge of clergymen who had slipped from the path of sobriety. Dolling complained rather pathetically at Poplar that 'the people who send these cases never offer any money; they seem to think I have a gold-mine of my own, or a magnet to dig into other people's. Those in authority in the Church of England have no method for helping such cases, and that is the reason why so many scandals exist.'

Soldiers and Sailors were always in and out of the Parsonage at Portsmouth. The town was full of temptations, and their homes were often far away. More often still they had no homes to go to, and some of the boys of the *St. Vincent* always spent their holidays with Dolling. Sometimes a soldier or sailor would drop in after an absence of two or three years, make the Parsonage his home as long as his furlough lasted, and then be off again to the other end of the world. They didn't write letters in their absence, sailors rarely write, but St. Agatha's was their home, and it was Dolling's joy to make his house a home for the homeless. A Colonel in the Guards, who knew Dolling well, said of him when he died, 'He knew a soldier's feelings as he did those of other men, and there was no one we sent to him who did not get sympathy.'

It was only natural that a good number of those who sought out Dolling were comparatively worthless characters, mere wasters of the substance of others. Sometimes they were 'escaped monks' from Roman Catholic monasteries who turned out to be people of very unsavoury reputations. Dolling found these men who wanted to change their religion the worst of all the shady persons who came to him.

Then there were men who wanted to be clergymen, of thought they were called to the religious life. Others came because they had heard of the ritual in the church. Dolling had a short way of testing their earnestness. He had a lot of books before he sold his library, and his plan was to get a duster and bid them dust the books and catalogue them. A very few days at this cataloguing were enough for most of them, and they found excuses for departing.

But for the poor wreckage of humanity Dolling's sympathy never failed. When he left Portsmouth and was himself without permanent home or work, he wrote:

'I take them out of my heart where some of them have lain for eight long years. I take them out one by one – thieves, felons, tramps, loafers, outcasts, of whom the world was not worthy, having no place for them, no home for them, no work for them. I read in their eyes a tenderness, and in their hearts a compassion for me, a bearing with all my ill-temper, and paying me back a hundredfold in the richest coin of truest love.'

This rare compassion was not for men more than for women. Dolling hated the glib talk that treated fallen womanhood as a necessity for men who must needs sow 'wild oats.' 'When society is brave enough to say a "fallen man," as well as a "fallen woman," the so-called fallen woman will soon disappear,' he declared.

And so while he waged war against the proprietors of bad houses and got these houses shut up, his sisters and their friends opened their doors and their hearts to the hapless women who were turned out. If the Parsonage welcomed the men of broken lives, in Miss Dolling's love there was a shelter for all unhappy women. The ordinary 'Penitentiary' (the very name is discouraging), with its rules and its cold, chilling, utterly unsympathetic atmosphere, Dolling knew, could not do the work that was wanted. 'These institutions,' he used to say, 'treat the girl as if she was created for the Home instead of the Home being created for the girl. And that's the worst of all institutions, with their rules and officials.'

He understood, too, that though the body may be defiled and wrecked, heroic and beautiful qualities may still lurk in the soul. One Sunday night when he preached in St. Paul's Cathedral he told a story (which he often told elsewhere) of his early work in East London. He had been informed of a girl lying very ill in his parish, and he climbed the rickety staircase of a slum lodging-house to find her. The room was at the top, and the sick woman shared it with her friend; they were both of the same unfortunate occupation, earning a few pence every night on the streets. The girls was very ill; the exposure and hard life had worn her out, and she was friendless but for her companion. The other girl opened the door to Dolling, and she had pawned her ulster – it was the only thing pawnable left – to buy a little brandy for her friend. Without her ulster it was impossible to ply her trade on the streets, but she had given her all for her friend, though starvation stared her in the face. She had done what she could. Dolling looked down on the great congregation under the dome of the Cathedral that Sunday night and told the story. Then he added: 'Is there one of us here to night in all this respectable and religious assembly who would make so great a sacrifice as that poor girl made for her friend?'

Father Dolling has passed away; no more on earth is there room in his heart for the outcasts and homeless. Many of the clergy whom he saved will pray for him till the day of their death, and those on whose lips words of prayer rarely come still bless him in their lives.

But the open house has gone, the common sacramental meal for the weary and heavy-laden is no longer spread, and men and women lie bruised and wounded by the roadside in this England without hope of any Samaritan to heal them.

Good priests and faithful shepherds abound. Where is the heart that beats for the sheep who are far from any fold, the strong love that cannot rest while men and women perish? To all whom he saved Robert Dolling left a legacy, the care of the homeless and outcast. As he had restored them, so, too, is it their work to restore others.

CHAPTER IX

DOLLING'S VIEWS ON THE THEATRE AND AMUSEMENT

Dolling had a very real affection for the theatre. Anything that filled up a large place in the public mind interested him, and his love for life itself and for the beautiful in life – a love he nourished and cultivated to the end – took him often to the theatre, and made him a dramatic critic of no mean ability. A keen scent for the beautiful, a sound judgment in matters of taste, and a simple enjoyment of good art, are the notes of Dolling's attitude to the theatre. He never had any notion of 'reconciling' church and stage, or preaching and actors and actresses. His friends were on the stage as they were elsewhere, his 'spiritual children' – danced, sang, and acted with his full and enthusiastic benediction.

Mrs. Crowe, whose father first brought out Henry Irving at the Lyceum, and whom an earlier generation of playgoers knew as Miss Bateman, and her two sisters, Mrs. Edward Compton and Miss Isabelle Bateman (who left the stage to enter the Church of England Sisterhood), were Dolling's friends for over twenty-five years.

Whilst he lay dying at his sister's house in Philbeach Gardens, someone told him that an old Wykehamist, Mr. Paul Rubens, was just bringing out a new piece, 'Three

Little Maids', at a West-End theatre and Dolling at once sent a message of 'good luck.' It was entirely characteristic of him that he shared the joys of his friends as well as their sorrows,

Of recent years the demands upon his time by the needs of Poplar left Dolling few opportunities for the theatre. At Portsmouth he was a regular playgoer, and the first time I visited St. Agatha's on a Saturday night in December, 1887, I had to pass from the Parsonage to the crowded Pit of the Old Theatre to find Father Dolling. Osborne, his curate, was with him; they were both enjoying Edward Compton's Company in 'The Road to Ruin.'

Dolling believed in the Spirit of God manifest in the world, a Spirit that cleansed and renewed. Novelty and change never frightened of shocked him. In religion, politics, art, he welcomed the new spirit. And so the dramas of Ibsen interested him enormously. When 'The Doll's House,' 'Hedda Gabler,' and 'Little Eyolf' were performed in London and the ordinary dramatic critics and the average playgoer, puzzled and confused by unusual and unexpected demands on the intelligence, pronounced against Ibsen, Dolling at once recognised the truth and power of the great Scandinavian's message, and found these plays – the only three he saw performed on the stage – of deep and valuable and moral significance. The wonderful acting of Mrs. Charrington (Miss Janet Achurch), Miss Robins, and Mrs. Patrick Campbell impressed him, and he insisted on its greatness. At the very time when certain fatuous people were declaring Ibsen's 'Little Eyolf' to be immoral and crowding the theatre to see 'The Geisha,' Dolling, who knew from his many sailor friends the purposes of a Japanese tea-house, was lost in indignant amazement. For the popular 'musical comedy,' with its cheap tunes, its vulgarity, its jesting on matrimonial infidelities, its stale, immoral treatment of sex, its banal stupidities, he had no love.

'The Sign of the Cross' is a play that many church dignitaries and some dramatic critics have blessed, a play that has enjoyed considerable popularity. It was with difficulty that Dolling could sit through a performance of it. He shook off his boots and sat in his box restless and miserable when he was taken to see it. What distressed him was that at the very time when 'The Sign of the Cross' was setting out on its long and successful run, 'Michael and his Lost Angel' at the Lyceum was withdrawn after a very few nights. Dolling was moved by 'Michael and his Lost Angel' that he wanted to get up in the Lyceum and tell the audience what a splendid play it was. And, preaching at St. Matthias', Earl's Court, at that season, he did point out how a fine and true drama had been rejected by the public in favour of the shoddy common-place of 'The Sign of the Cross.' Dolling always wanted people to discern the moving of the Spirit of God in every manifestation of life, and in every new good play he saw such manifestation. Does this play make for good? Was his one question. Does it arouse the conscience, stimulate thought, move us to compassion or to heroism? Does it even send us home with a sense of recreation? Has it given us one good laugh at our follies? An answer in the affirmative was sufficient to stamp the piece as approved by God. An appreciation of Ibsen did not in the least prevent an honest enjoyment of a rollicking farce. The need for laughter is so great – and Dolling knew that tired and earnest people are apt to find so few occasions for mirth. He felt, too, that without a sense of humour earnest and hard-working people often become dull, insensitive, and unsympathetic, and their labours fruitless. So Dolling always enjoyed such absurdities as the 'Pantomime Rehearsal' and 'The Magistrate,' and declared they did him good. Sometimes he would laugh so much that even the actors became embarrassed. At a burlesque of Mr. Henry Arthur Jones' 'Bauble Shop' – a piece called the 'Babble Shop' – it was soon withdrawn and probably few London playgoers remember it) – Dolling's laughter moved Mr. Arthur Playfair to send a message of remonstrance from the stage. And the same thing happened at a performance of 'The Magistrate' at the Old Court Theatre at Sloane Square, when Mr. John Clayton declared he really couldn't act, because Dolling, who was in a box near the stage, would laugh so hugely.

But it had to be good, honest fun to provoke Dolling's laughter. It didn't matter how absurd and noisy the fun if it was clean. Music-halls bored and saddened him, and he never went to them unless his boys made him take them. On one occasion Dolling, tired and not interested, dropped asleep in a London music-hall and fell off his seat, thereby provoking the rebuke from the attendant that it was disgraceful for a clergyman to behave like that in a public place of entertainment. Italian opera and oratorios did not move him; he found them altogether too long, and went to sleep at an Albert Hall performance of the 'Messiah' as easily as he did at a music-hall.

The recent plays of Mr. Stephen Philips – 'Paolo and Francesca' and 'Herod' – appealed to Dolling's sense of beauty and won his admiration. So strong was his belief in the need for recreation through the stage that as a clergyman he always did what he could to provide visits to the theatre for the people of his parish. He would persuade managers to give him free tickets to a pantomime for his Sunday-school children and mothers' meetings. At Poplar, even more than at Portsmouth, the gray monotony of the lives around him made Dolling cleave to the theatre. In an article in St. Saviour's parish magazine in 1899 he put this plainly:

'I am quite sure that if we measure the character of Jesus Christ, the first thing He would have done here would have been to have fed the hungry, and to have piped to the people that they might dance, till He had exorcised the numbness which poverty and dullness always produce. He could not have otherwise touched that Divine spark, the likeness of God, which is in us by right of our creation in His image.' Further on in the same article are these words: 'If we can realize more of the spirit of joy, we shall have learnt to realize more of the Kingdom of God.'

In the first annual report of the work at Poplar there is the same plea for amusement from Dolling's pen, and a glowing account of a parochial visit to a theatre:

'Shortly after Christmas I was able to take them all (the mothers' meeting) to the pantomime at Dalston. Mr. Compton, the lessee, gave us very cheap tickets, and the railway fare did not come to much. I doubt if 200 people ever had a better time at such a little cost. But here again one realized the awful dullness of their life. The majority of them had never been to a place of amusement before. I wish you could have heard them laugh. What a debt we owe to the lessees of good suburban theatres; they are in the truest sense, ministers of God. Those who can afford it *will* have amusement. How we ought to bless God for anybody who can let them have that amusement wholesome and clean! And yet the case of those who never can have amusement seems almost worse. Think of a woman's life here: an enormous family, one continuous struggle to provide not that which is sufficient, but what will keep body and soul together for even if the husband earns a little money everything depends on her, every meal cooked by herself, hardly ever able to sit down and rest. The men all have some variety in life; she has none.'

'I think we need some good place of entertainment down her,' was one comment on the parish of St. Saviour's Poplar, made by its Vicar in 1899.

If Dolling accounted the theatre a means of grace, dancing was no less honourable in his eyes. He declared it to be 'in itself a great educational power.' And said that a beautiful ballet must appeal to all that was true and noble in the heart of man. Dancing classes were instituted by him at Portsmouth and Poplar, as Bible-classes are instituted in other parishes, and his testimony to the class at Portsmouth was that 'for the last five years our dancing-class has been one of the most valuable parish institutions.'

Dolling also wrote at greater length on the importance of a dancing-class from the clergyman's standpoint:

'Everyone pays twopence, and we dance from 8 till 10.30 p.m. It is extraordinary the difference which this has effected in the manners of our people. The dancing is, perhaps, a little more serious than at a ball in Belgravia, for

117

squares are danced with a due attention to the figures. It has given one the most happy opportunity of enabling our boys and girls to meet naturally together, and I am more and more convinced by experience that one of the greatest causes of sin in places like ours is this want. Many of our boys and girls have got engaged to be married through this chance, and if any one of them get engaged to a girl outside the parish, the dance gives them an excellent excuse to introduce her to us. It would be very difficult to say "You must come and my parson." It is very easy to say, "You must come and see my dancing-class." In the last six years I do not think we have had one marriage amongst our people for which we have had cause to feel shame. In the last four years I do not think any of our people have been married without receiving the Holy Communion on the Sunday before, or on the morning of their marriage.'

At Poplar dancing-classes were a strong feature of the social work of the parish, and with equally good results.

It must not be thought, however, that Dolling established dancing-classes in order to attract people to church. He established dancing-classes because he believed dancing to be good and because he refused to recognise hard-and-fast lines dividing the secular from the religious. 'Who can separate the secular from the religious?' Dolling once wrote in an article in the *Church Review*. 'Certainly the Master did not try to do so. And the reason is obvious: "That which God hath joined together let no *man* put asunder."'

A tiny girl, who dances beautifully and whom Dolling loved, said, one day, 'When I dance my feet are laughing.' This laughter of the feet, this poetry of motion, as others

118

have called it, was then a manifestation of life which Dolling held to be of God.

Painting and sculpture appealed to Dolling less – movement and colour in life satisfied the artist in him. But he knew a good picture and the importance of good decorative art in church and schools, and on holidays on the Continent spent hours in public galleries.

Dolling was never a scholar, but he read widely and with real pleasure in the odd times snatched from preaching and parochial engagements, and his opinion on books were as sound as his opinion on plays. Osborne, his senior curate at Portsmouth, read theology and Browning with him of a morning for some years, and in his last days on earth he would have Mrs. Crowe to read to him. Long railway journeys gave opportunity for reading. Dolling had a remarkable way of getting at the heart of a book very quickly; he could pick out the vital parts with the speed and accuracy of a practised reviewer. In literature it seemed to him there was scanty token of a new spirit at work, and very few modern novels pleased him. George Meredith's great novels and Mr. Rudyard Kipling's stories remained a joy to him, though he would not accept Mr. Kipling's 'Absent-minded Beggar' as a typical soldier; and he professed himself never tired of Miss Charlotte Yonge's tales, especially the 'Pillars of the House.' 'They are so wholesome,' he would say.

The power and originality of Walt Whitman's 'Leaves of Grass' impressed Dolling, and he acknowledged it. It was natural that robust, virile literature should move him, and all Whitman's 'Love of Comrades' was his. He could say with Whitman:

'I have given alms to everyone that asked;
Stood up for the stupid and crazy; devoted my income and
    labour to others;
    Gone freely with powerful, uneducated persons, and
with the
    young and with the mothers of families.'

It was 'Underneath all, individuals' with Dolling, too –
always the building up of persons, not the success of
Church or State, was his main concern.

Maeterlinck's 'Wisdom and Destiny' was a book that
Dolling appreciated very highly. He read it closely and gave
it to many of his friends; and, of course, Charles Dickens
was always one of his favourite authors.

Unlike many devout Churchmen, Dolling never used
books of devotion. The Bible he knew well, read constantly,
and loved. But the little pious books that find such a
market in Anglo-Catholic circles he couldn't stand.

'Ready-made prayers,' said Father Stanton in a
sermon at St. Alban's one Sunday, 'are like ready-made
clothes. We may try and make them fit us, but we know
they are not really ours, and they never quite fit.'

Dolling felt that about all manuals of religion. He
had to make his own devotions, other people's prayers
never really suited him. That was the secret of his
'disloyalty' to the formularies of the Church of England. He
couldn't find the Book of Common Prayer sufficient. The
most beautiful of the ancient collects didn't always fit. He
must pray in his own words, pouring out his soul on behalf
of his people in the language that the Spirit moved him to

use. He never gave up extempore prayer in church, and it was one of the points on which he came into collision with the late Bishop of Winchester.

The Bible was his great Book. He was grounded in it as John Ruskin was, and knew it through and through. The Higher Criticism and the scientific research into the dates and question of authorship of the books of the bible never touched Dolling's love for the Scriptures nor affected his point of view. It was a great literature given by God to the world, full of wisdom, comfort, and help for man: as such Dolling accepted the Bible, and the matters in dispute did not interest him.

CHAPTER X

AFTER PORTSMOUTH AND A YEAR IN AMERICA

For fifteen months after Father Dolling left Portsmouth he was without regular work in England. Bishops looked shyly upon him, and in two dioceses refused him permission to preach. Dr. Westcott declined to give him leave to conduct a mission in Durham, and Dr. Perowne was equally prohibitive as far as Worcester was concerned. But he was very busy all the same, preaching wherever he was invited, and devoting the collections made after his sermons to the Winchester College Mission. He knew money was needed at Landport, and though his responsibility for the debts at St. Agatha's had ceased, and though he was no more to minister there, he could not help begging for the Mission.

On St. Agatha's Day, February, 1896, he gathered round him in London many of his old workers at Portsmouth, and preached to them at St. Cuthbert's Church, Earl's Court. One sentence in that sermon still rings out clearly: 'The principle of love is the only one which in the end succeeds.' With all the getting and giving of money, amid all disputes and controversies, Dolling built his work on the sure foundation, on this principle of love.

The following Lent he preached incessantly, delivering ten courses every week, and no less than fifteen sermons in the first week, and all this necessarily meant spending a great deal of time in railway-trains and very scanty leisure. He still made some attempt to keep open house, too, though he had no house of his own. His home was at his sister's place in Wetherby Mansions, Earl's Court, in those days, and he would often bring in stray friends to dinner there.

As the months went by and no one offered him permanent work, his eyes were turned towards America. Dolling made allowance for the absence of any appointment, writing with characteristic generosity when he was in America: 'It is not always easy for Bishops or patrons, however desirous, to find a living suited for such an irregular person as myself, and therefore I don't feel the least hurt that I was not offered permanent work before I left England.'

Two posts, indeed were offered to him. Dr. Marshall invited him to take up the chaplaincy of St. Raphael's, near Bristol, and the ministry of an episcopal church near Glasgow was suggested. In neither place was there scope for Dolling's energy: at St. Raphael's the chief business was to minister to a convent of religious women, and in Scotland he would have been isolated from active life. Beyond a holiday in the spring of 1896, Dolling continued his itinerant preaching, however, and a large number of pulpits were placed at his disposal. He was in demand, too, for meetings of the English Church Union and the Christian Social Union.

In the early part of the year, 'in the odd moments seized out of a very busy Lent,' Dolling wrote the 'Ten Years in a Portsmouth Slum,' and the book was published by

Messrs. Swan Sonnenschien in the following May. The charm and simplicity of this story of Dolling's work at Portsmouth achieved distinct and marked success, and the 'Ten Years' ran through five editions in less than two years. It fully deserved its popularity. Every page bears the impress of Dolling's personality and 'whoso touches this book touches a man.' Perhaps it will be brought out again; there must be room for a new, cheap edition now, and it has been out of print for a considerable time. We often wanted Dolling to publish other writings, especially some of his sermons, and he did talk about doing it. But the task, was put off, and now all that could be done would be to gather up in a little volume some collection of the sermons, addresses, and articles of his that have appeared in various newspapers and magazines.

The Dean and Chapter of St. Paul's were anxious to keep Dolling in England in that year of uncertainty. He preached in the Cathedral, when certain Bishops frowned upon him; and they would have given him the Vicarage of St. Mary, Somers Town, but for an unfortunate provision that required the incumbent to have spent six years in London as a clergyman before he could be appointed.

In the Lent of 1897, just before he left for America, Dolling preached, on the invitation of Canon Eyton, a remarkable course of sermons at St. Margaret's Church, Westminster. 'The East-End Loafer,' 'The West-End Loafer,' 'The Prostitute,' 'The Society that Breeds Them,' 'The Church that does not Save Them,' were the titles of these addresses. The daily murder and waste of body and soul in the Metropolis was the burden of the series.

I take from Dolling's rough notes some thoughts he dwelt on. Wrong economic conditions, false social views, caused the defacement of God's image, and the Church 'passed by on the other side.' The majority of East-End loafers had never had a chance; environment and heredity were against them at birth; want of food and discipline had reduced the physical man till he was unable to face hard work. Yet they were our brothers still and God's children.

So also were the West-End loafers, in the making of whom, in like manner, heredity and environment played its part. And if there were fewer loafers in West-end clubs and parks, it was because they were so much more expensive than their brothers of East London. The ideal of honour and the ideal of work have been so largely lost among the rich, that was the root of the trouble. Old-fashioned ideas of responsibility and conceptions of duty were voted out of date, and the lust of pleasure and excitement was fashionable. The old age of the loafer, if he lived to be old, was a loveless thing.

The Prostitute was never amongst the unemployed; she had always herself – the image and Temple of the Eternal God – to sell. And the man of the world without any thought of the result, bought her. False standards of morality let the man go free, and condemned the woman to life-long hell; and Justice and Compassion alone could restore her.

Our society was not Christian, the principles of Christ were not the national ideals in home, or foreign matters. Olive Schreiner's book, 'Trooper Peter Halkett,' was a terrible indictment of English methods in South Africa. British 'interest' were preferred before British honour. Mammon was the great god in London, and in his service there was no freedom for capitalist or workmen.

The Church passes by the fallen. In the slums and on tramp men and women live and die without religion. Since the Reformation the Church has been lost to the masses. It had ceased to touch the lives of people. Its services were liked by the respectable middle-class, but did not minister to the needs of the majority. Its clergy were drawn from the Universities, and men of enthusiasm and devotion were rejected by Bishops in favour of some utterly incompetent graduate. Dissenters, Roman Catholics, and the Salvation Army touched the hearts of people where the Church of England failed. The clergy wanted to do the right thing, but they did not understand the people nor the people them. The clergyman's life in his freehold vicarage was so remote from the lives of his people, and the lack of sympathy and imagination kept him aloof. The Bishops were still more cut off from the slums. But if the Church failed, Christ could never fail. He would yet draw all men unto Himself.

Can these rough notes convey anything of the force of the sermons? Only the people who heard them know their searching and stirring character. Mr. John Burns, M.P., was in the large and strangely assorted audience that gathered at St. Margaret's Church in the March days of 1897, and recently he recalled the occasion.

'Father Dolling,' he said, 'was one of the very few clergymen I could listen to with interest and pleasure. The impression he made upon me by a sermon he preached in St. Margaret's, Westminster, some years ago on behalf of the poor and the outcast still remains with me. He was so human, and now he has killed himself with work.'

Dolling never preached more effectively then in those fifteen months when he was out of work, and he collected a large sum of money for St. Agatha's. Some of his 'children' wanted help, too, and he could not bear that any whom he knew and loved should starve.

But despite all this preaching, no one would give him a church to minister in, a parish to govern, or a mission to undertake. At times he wondered whether there was any sphere for him in the Church of England as a priest. Not that he thought of becoming a Roman Catholic, still less of starting a church of his own – though this was once proposed to him by a friend to whom apostolical succession and Church order were of no account. But it did seem to Dolling that he would be obliged to earn a living at some secular work, if the Church refused to employ him.

However, he determined to go to America first. The American Episcopal Church was not 'established,' and it would surely be more free and tolerant. Besides, he needed a holiday, and so at the end of May he sailed for the United States.

Both the Bishop of Winchester and the Bishop of Rochester gave him letters of recommendation to the American Episcopate, and Dr. Fearon, the Headmaster of Winchester, wrote most warmly of the work at Portsmouth and Winchester. Dr. Randall Davidson described the Rev. R. R. Dolling as 'a priest of irreproachable moral character, and of remarkable earnestness, devotion and capacity,' and added: 'I gladly testify to my profound respect for the devoted work he has done in this Diocese and I entertain for Mr. Dolling personally a very sincere regard.'

Dr. Talbot, who had made some endeavour, without success, to find some sphere of work in Deptford for the ex-missioner of Landport, declared: 'Mr. Dolling's work is well known in the Church; it has been an example in her midst of what profound desire to witness and convey God's love to the poorest of His people may accomplish when expressed by a life of entire self-sacrifice, in the spirit of brotherly fellowship, with every sort and condition of man, and in the full use of the means of grace.'

It may be asked, If the Bishops of Winchester and Rochester thought so highly of Dolling, why did they not give him work in their dioceses? And the only answer is in Dolling's own words: 'It is not always easy for Bishops or patrons, however desirous, to find a living for such an irregular person as myself.'

The visit to America was a complete success. Dolling liked the United States: he enjoyed the movement and life, the large scale on which things were done, the freedom of social intercourse, the excitement and rush. And America liked him; his frankness won the American. The newspapers boomed him, large audiences came to hear him preach, and he was entertained with lavish hospitality. Of course, he found and made many friends in the States, but one house more than any other was his place of rest and recreation. With Mrs. Stevens and her sons at Castle Point, New York, he made his home, and when Mrs. Stevens died, within a year of Dolling's return to England he wrote: 'I went to America very despondent, very downhearted. It is to Castle Point that I owe all my recovery.'

Many of the boys whom Dolling had emigrated from East London and Portsmouth welcomed him. Almost the first day he arrived in Philadelphia a big man came into his room, and when Dolling asked him who he was, he explained how Dolling had emigrated him from the North of Ireland twenty-six years before, and was almost annoyed at not being recognised. In Philadelphia alone he found twenty of his boys, all doing well.

Dolling's sermons drew the Americans even more than they did English people. He travelled a great deal, and preached in New York, Boston, Philadelphia, Washington, Chicago, Buffalo, Utica, St. Louis, Minneapolis, and many other places. Early in 1898 he crossed over into Canada and conducted a mission at New Brunswick. Altogether Dolling preached over 600 sermons during the year he spent in America, and conducted several missions and conferences, and he came back to England feeling younger and stronger than when he left. Of course, he begged money during those twelve months, and, of course, it was for Portsmouth. The Infant Schools at St. Agatha's needed rebuilding, and Dolling laboured hard to get money for them. To his great satisfaction they were reopened free of debt in February, 1898.

Much as he enjoyed the travelling and the preaching, Dolling wanted to settle down somewhere in a parish of his own. He still thought of England, and waited hopefully for recall, but as months passed and no recall came, he decided that he would take whatever permanent work was offered to him, whether in England or America. And then, on March 28, 1898, came a letter from Mr. Chandler, the Rector of Poplar, offering him the Vicarage of St. Saviour's, and Dolling cabled acceptance at once. A few hours afterwards the Bishop of Chicago asked him to be Dean of Chicago Cathedral, and the same night St. Margaret's Church, Aberdeen, was offered to him. The next morning he heard that he could have a church at Nottingham.

For more than two years Dolling had been wandering, and now four different livings were offered to him within twenty-four hours. Poplar had been accepted, and so, after fulfilling his engagements in America, Dolling set sail for England. He landed in July, and went at once to St. Saviour's. 'I have been living in the sunshine,' he said, 'and it has got into my bones and into my marrow.' In a very few years the sunshine had passed from his body, and bones and marrow returned to the dust from whence they came.

CHAPTER XI

FOUR YEARS AT POPLAR

On Friday evening, July 22, 1898, Robert Radclyffe Dolling was formally instituted to the Vicarage of St. Saviour's, Poplar, London, by the Bishop of Stepney (Dr. Winnington Ingram), acting for the Bishop of London, and on the following Sunday morning Dolling 'read himself in' – that is he read the Thirty-nine Articles of the Prayer-Book at the morning service. The congregation, chiefly composed of Sunday-school children listened with patience to the reading.

A protest made against the appointment on the ground of Dolling's ritualism at Portsmouth was not taken too seriously. A gentleman in the congregation came forward on the Bishop's inquiry at the Service of Institution if there was any objection to the institution of Robert Radclyffe Dolling, and quietly read a complaint concerning Dolling's alleged 'heresy' at St. Agatha's, Portsmouth. The Bishop listened, assured the objector that the Bishop of London was fully aware of Mr. Dolling's career, and the service proceeded. In the vestry after the service, Dolling, with characteristic ease, invited the objector to come and have a cup of tea; 'it is such a very hot night,' he added. In the parish magazine the objection is alluded to very briefly by the new Vicar:

'You did not seem to mind – and I am sure I did not – the objection lodged by some Mr. Hill, though I think we ought to be grateful to him for being very courteous and polite in what he did, and as far as I am concerned, and, I hope, as far as you are concerned, we shall always treat all outside interference with exactly the same indifference. When I have any complaint to make of you, you may be quite sure I shall not be backward in making it, both in the pulpit and out of the pulpit. I know that you cannot come into the pulpit and complain of me, but I earnestly trust that, if there is anything I say or do that you do not understand, you will come and tell me straight, so that we may talk it out together, and, above all, pray over it.'

That was always Dolling's attitude to outside criticism. He had far too much sense of humour to be disturbed by any 'church crisis' concerning ritual.

'The REAL CRISIS,' he wrote in February, 1899, 'the one that ought to make all Churchmen, cleric or laic, on their knees in penitence before God, confess their negligence, is that the vast majority of English people care nothing for the Church, many even nothing for God. If we learn this lesson, then all the present distress is cheaply purchased.'

Dolling was never really happy at Poplar. It was a heavy task to be sent at the age of forty-seven, with health impaired by ten years at Portsmouth, to take charge of 'the grayest, dullest parish in London.' The absence of movement and colour depressed him. Portsmouth, with all its horrors, was much more alive. Then Uppingham School, which had been interested in St. Saviour's withdrew its support on Dolling's appointment. His sisters, and Miss

Blair and Miss Rowan, who had shared the work at Portsmouth and Maidment Street, came to St. Saviour's and remained to the end. Dolling gave up the Vicarage to them, and lived in a Clergy House, built over the schools. Here is his own account of the parish of St. Saviour's, Poplar, in July, 1898.

'This parish covers forty-four acres, and contains 10,000 people, so we are all packed very close together. If people are like parish churches, this ought to make us very friendly and very religious, for the closer a church is packed, the more friendly the intercourse, the more fervent the worship. We are equally distant from our two great thoroughfares, the Burdett Road and the East India Dock Road – about an eighth of a mile – and the streets between us are small and sordid, so that we shall not be bothered by outsiders.'

The income was £220 a year, and £450 was needed for the salaries of three curates.

Dolling grasped the conditions of life around him at once. In the following September he writes in his parish magazine: 'I think that it is a very lucky thing that I and my sisters have been here in August, for I hope it will teach us to understand the difficulties under which so many of you have to live in this place. We, at any rate, have large rooms, and are not overcrowded; I was going to say also we have plenty of water, but that is not quite true, for in the Mission House the flow is uncertain. But the following table enables me to know in what close quarters most of you have to live:

Description of House.	No.	Adults.	Children.	W.C.	Taps
13 rooms	3	13	4	6	10
10 "	2	15	6	3	4
9 "	2	13	4	2	5
8 "	27	154	84	28	50
7 "	56	297	160	58	71
6 "	649	3,091	2,141	659	809
5 "	157	682	553	169	186
4 "	200	765	571	200	235
3 "	6	15	4	6	6
2 "	2	4	6	2	2
	-------	-------	-------	-------	-------
	1,104	5,049	3,533	1,133	1,378
		8,582			

'I quite understand how the high price of rents necessitates this manner of living. No one except yourselves deplores that more than I do, for I foresee how almost impossible it will be for us to get land to add some kind of working plant to the parish. When I see your children forced to play in the streets because there, except the Poplar Recreation Ground difficult to reach, and not always a desirable place for little girls to play in; when I know that, with the exception of a few houses in one street, there are no baths in the Parish, and the Poplar Baths are expensive and overcrowded, and that therefore needed washing is a great difficulty; when I know that our lads, so that they may be able to play football, have to pay eight shillings for the use of a ground for the afternoon, as well as threepence railway fare there and back, day by day I marvel more and more, and bless God for the buoyancy of your spirits and the cheerfulness of your hope.

'This surely only entails upon me more and more the duty of trying to make our life as liveable as possible. Living within a stone's throw of "Stink House Bridge," and with the salubrious Limehouse Cut one of the boundaries of our Parish, we cannot expect that the air we breathe shall be always the best. But surely we have a right to demand that the water we consume shall be so, both in quantity and quality.'

The East London Water Famine in the summer of 1898 meant, of course, very serious discomfort to Dolling and his parishioners. But we have referred to this matter elsewhere.

It was amid these surroundings and conditions, then, that Dolling set to work at St. Saviour's, Poplar. It was his last parish, and after nearly four years he gave up his charge at the call of death.

Of course, money was wanted. There was rebuilding to be done for the schools. 'I value my schools more than anything else in my parish,' Dolling wrote, 'but I have no hesitation in saying that if I could not make them wholesome, I should deem it my duty to close them.' That they needed very thorough overhauling was indisputable.

'On the ground-floor the boys and infants are placed; over the boys the girls; and over the infants the house that I and my assistants and anyone who comes to live with us will occupy. In the centre of all this is a small back-yard, which contains all the offices of the boys and infants, and they are evidently in a bad state. The windows of the School and of our own dwelling, which look upon this yard, can consequently never be opened, which results in very bad ventilation. I must pull all these offices down, and rebuild them in the playground. By far the most important matter in a densely populated place like ours are good drains. I deem it necessary, both for our own health and that of the children, that this should be done at once. A sweet and clean School is the larger part of a good education in a place like this, and a well-ventilated and well-drained house a positive necessity for clergy and workers.'

Over £3,000 was spent on rebuilding and repairing the schools, and this £3,000 is only a small part of the sum collected by Dolling in the four years at Poplar. Increased attendances and bigger grants were a satisfactory return for the improvements in the schools.

The open house, which had been so great a feature of the life at Portsmouth, was maintained at St. Saviour's, and now Miss Dolling and the ladies who worked with her in the parish also sat at the common board. At St. Agatha's Parsonage it was only open house for men and boys.

Of course, Dolling gathered all sorts and conditions of men into his house. Distressed and out-of-work clergymen, young men of uncertain vocation, the weak and homeless, and theological students. It will never be known how many clergymen, fallen from grace, were restored to health and work by the discipline of residence in Dolling's house. And when it is said, and with truth, that the only class of people of whom Dolling spoke habitually with harshness and contempt were his brother clergy, let it always be remembered that there are many clergymen to-day in the Church of England who came to Dolling, broken and fallen men, whom no one else would bear with, and whom the authorities despaired of; and that with patience, tenderness, and strength he healed them and sent them out again to their work, renewed and cleansed.

Dolling writes of some of the people in his Clergy House at St. Saviour's in September, 1899.

'Then I want to emigrate a very promising young man to South Africa; he is just cut out for one of the police forces out there, but circumstances have been against him in this country; and another lad to Canada; and to pay six guineas fees for a boy at a Typewriting and Shorthand College; and I especially want £40 for two years for the fees of a young man to go to King's College.

'I could go on multiplying this list without ceasing. There are always about twenty-four of us – clergy, women, lay-workers, and those being helped. Any housekeeper, or any man who pays a housekeeper's bills, can guess what this means. But this gospel of food and good-fellowship, and learning compassion and forbearance, is beyond all price, and anybody who said to me, "I will give you 15s. a week," would enable me to add another scholar to the School. There are homeless ones who have never had a home; there are more homeless ones who have had one and lost it. Sometimes I think that from want of thought people take all their food, and clothes, and home comforts just as a matter of course, and almost cease to feel any thanksgiving for them. Don't you think they would realize all this much more if only they could, when they say their grace, or when they bless God morning and evening, for all they have, just think of some such place as this, where I have to strive so hard and pray so unceasingly for what they are, from very continual use, in a great danger of wasting, and how over and over again my heart almost breaks at having to say, "I cannot help you." Go up into your nurseries, look at your little children in bed, eagerly watch for the post which brings you the first letter on the return to school, and, when your heart is full of thankfulness and your eyes are full of tears, say, "There were fathers and mothers who cried and rejoiced over little children. Those children to-day are men and women, helpless, hopeless, alone, and, if it were not for God's grace, so may mine be, so may mine be."'

Who could resist such an appeal? Not the kind, wealthy people whom Dolling addressed, and money came in freely for the various works in Poplar.

Schools, clubs, the common-table, the purchase of houses for the curates and parish workers, coals, dinners for the sick, food-tickets, parochial charities and entertainments, all meant money and necessitated a large income.

With that wonderful frankness which was always in him Dolling said with truth, 'Money actually represents souls to me.'

Of his charities he wrote in March 1901:

'What we spend in charity, though it seems to be very large, goes in sick-dinners, food-tickets, and in the hundred other things that the district visitors, under Miss Dolling's most careful supervision, dispense. If you only knew the needs of a place like this, you would realize how very little we spend. Here is a widow, with an epileptic daughter and no support except by mangling. Here another woman supports five children by her washing, one girl only working, a husband always ill. Here a widow, the elder girl earning 8s.; six others to support by making match-boxes at 2½d. a gross. Even that is slack at times. Here a mother, the husband in a lunatic asylum, earns about 8s. a week; the elder girl earns 7s.; four other children in school. In every one of these cases a real struggle to be respectable. Here a man crawled to his work as long as he was able to, now broken down by rheumatism, the wife struggling to keep him alive.... Then, as cases to be helped get on our hands, expenses increase enormously. I am responsible now for £2 a week for a poor priest who has had to go to Bethlehem Hospital through no fault of his own. A lad, whose parents have just died, on the very verge of going to the bad, because he had to sleep out for three or four days, cost only a few shillings. He is now well placed, earning 10s. a week. A young Italian, stranded in this country, has taught himself English so well that on April 1 he goes to a good situation. These cases could be multiplied to any extent almost, for we are often a family of twenty living together.... And this, of course, explains and is an excuse for, the £800 that go for Mission expenses, by far the larger part of which is spent on the actual cost of our living, for I am almost led to suppose now we keep an unique house.'

To collect money for the expenses of Poplar, Dolling went away preaching a great deal, chiefly in the West End of London. Sometimes he would speak to a large drawing-room audience on the needs of his parish. The incessant travelling and preaching really wore him out.

It must be remembered, too, that his house at Poplar was very far from comfortable, and he was fifty years old. Three months before he died he wrote pathetically of the want of proper accommodation for his guests, and of his personal discomfort. 'My own house is crammed, and yet we have to put some of our guests into other houses. Then my bedroom has no fireplace in it, and the top of my bed is in a chimney. The fireplace in my sitting-room is quite useless. We have no hot water or anything like that. I am quite sure if you saw me take my cold bath at 6 a.m. you would build me a proper house at once. But however willing you were you could not, because we cannot get any land.'

Often in Lent Father Dolling would preach three times a day. But he enjoyed it. Comparatively few people came to hear him at St. Saviour's, and Dolling liked to address large congregations and to move them to give him help. He believed it his mission to get money from the rich to give to the poor, and his success encouraged him to continue, even when his strength was passing from him. The burden of the poor and heavy-laden was always on him, and the more money he got for the relief of others the wider the vista of poverty became. No matter what his income might have been, Dolling would have found it insufficient for the wants of his neighbours and for the needs of his parish.

He begged over £5,000 in 1901, the last year at Poplar, and even then ended the year in debt and died a penniless man.

The response of the rich to Dolling's appeal for money was considerable. Those who subscribed to the Winchester College Mission and to St. Saviour's, Poplar, believed in Dolling and his work, and were not disappointed.

Here is a typical appeal issued by Dolling when he was preaching at Berkeley Chapel in the West End:

MAYFAIR! – POPLAR!

A GREATER CONTRAST THAN THIS DOES NOT EXIST IN THE WORLD

Everything here makes for Health and Happiness.
            Everything there makes for Sickness and Sorrow.

Here you have good houses, good air, open spaces, amusement, pleasure and plenty of money to buy everything you want; there we have bad houses, ill-drained, over-crowded; no open spaces; no baths; no amusement; no money. You are all going for a holiday; none of us can – unless someone pays for us.

God sent me down to Poplar to change all this, and I am doing the best I can. I have not got any money except what I beg from you. I am sending six hundred children into the country to spend a fortnight; I want £25 for five hundred Sunday-School children's outing; I want old clothes to dress my children in; in fact, I was everything and anything you could give me.

R. R. DOLLING.

Will you send some of these papers to your friends. Please subscribe to our *Magazine*- 2s. 6d. per year. Reading it is a liberal education in knowing how to help the poor.

It was from the fulness of his heart that Dolling spent himself and the money he collected on others. His parochial charities were never doles nor bribes. The common humanity of his neighbours touched him; he could not help helping them. No consideration of Church-membership or attendance limited his sympathies, and the sense of disappointment that the people of Poplar were not drawn to the Church at St. Saviour's, which at times saddened him, never entered into his plans of relief, nor hindered the succouring of a single person. Poplar, like the rest of industrial London, is not given to church-going, and neither the eloquence of Dolling nor his benevolence could change the habits of several generations.

He was 'Father' Dolling at St. Saviour's as he had been at Portsmouth and at St. Martin's Mission fifteen years before. The name 'Father' was given him, as he pointed out, when he was only a deacon, and therefore it had 'no theological significance.' It was not the title of 'Father' Dolling valued, but he did value much the thing. His ideal of a parish priest was to be the father of his flock, and in a very real sense he was always the father of the fatherless.

The people of Poplar, though they didn't listen to his sermons in church, understood that Dolling was their friend – that in any sorrow or distress they could count on his sympathy and help. And Dolling always knew that many who never sought his ministrations in church looked to him as 'Father,' and the knowledge cheered him, even when he was depressed at the scanty congregations in church.

Perhaps the most beneficial of the many philanthropic works at Poplar was the setting up of boys' camps and girls' camps at the seaside.

For the last four summers one of Dolling's wealthy friends has paid the expenses for a camp at Broadstairs, and for a month in the summer the boys of the parish school have had fresh air, sufficient food, and sea-bathing. Dolling always spent a good deal of time at this camp, and the headmaster and one of the clergy were there all the time.

But it wasn't enough to have boys' camp. In the summer of 1901 a girls' camp was established on Hayling Island, and sixty girls' spent holidays there under Miss Dolling's charge. This summer of 1902, though Dolling is dead, the laughter of the boys at Broadstairs camp and the splash of little feet on the shore at Hayling still sounds, and the children bless 'the Father' who sent them from the dingy streets of East London to play for a month in God's sunlight and to paddle in God's sea.

The outbreak of small-pox in 1901 meant a lot of work at St. Saviour's. Dolling believed in vaccination, and used every effort, in the face of opposition and indifference, to get his parishioners vaccinated. This meant coming into collision with the anti-vaccinators, a strong majority on the Poplar Board of Guardians; but Dolling never feared opposition, nor shrank from a fight. He believed vaccination to be a preventative from small-pox, and by speech and writing laboured to get the operation performed. He fought strenuously for the bodies and souls of his people at St. Saviour's; and now, when these streets of Poplar know him no more, and his voice sounds no more from the altar and pulpit of his Church, there lives in the neighbourhood the remembrance of the big, genial parson, who loved little children, and whose heart was in the joys and sorrows of his people.

CHAPTER XII

THE LAST ILLNESS AND THE PASSING OF FATHER DOLLING

In the autumn of 1901, after a little more than three years' work at St. Saviour's, Poplar, Dolling's health had utterly broken down, and the doctor insisted that he must go away to the baths at Aix-la-Chapelle for six weeks. Dolling did not want to go, but there was no help for it, and it seemed as if the waters at Aix and the fortnight's holiday afterwards in Belgium really restored him to health. He declared on his return that he was now quite well, that all his cares had been 'washed, rubbed, and electrified' out of him, that he felt 'twenty years younger,' and that 'all the people say I look it.' To complete the cure, the doctor forbad him to preach in Advent, 'a season when I always get a great deal of money,' Dolling remarked pathetically.

But the sickness that had come upon him was not to be displaced. At the beginning of 1902 Dolling felt so well he undertook a very heavy course of preaching for Lent, eight sets of sermons in different places, besides five addresses in St. Paul's Cathedral, and lantern lectures, and stray addresses. He wanted money to pay some parochial debt; but had there been no debt, Dolling would have wanted money just the same for the needs of the people of Poplar.

144

The weather was very bad in January and February, and the cold affected his chest. Still the preaching went on, and Dolling battled with the weariness that was fast overtaking him. He found himself unable to get up early every morning to celebrate Holy Communion, and obliged to stay in bed when he was not in the pulpit. To those who knew him intimately it was an ominous sign that he could no longer gather strength for that daily communion in church, a sign that the hour was approaching when man passes from the sacraments and symbols of his God to a clearer Presence. Then, when the cold was lessening in March, a drunken man trod on Dolling's foot at Tonbridge Station, when he was hurrying to catch a train, and the neglect of this injury necessitated the amputation of a toe. Dolling made light of this trouble: 'Luckily, I am so busy that I have not time to think of the pain' (he wrote), 'and all the time that I am pleading for my people, more and more I realize how small and contemptible my own ills are; for they bear the burden with extraordinary fortitude and courage, and my sisters and my lady-workers tell me it is impossible to imagine much of what they go through.'

In this same letter, the last he wrote from Poplar, he pleads with the rich for his own people at the East End: 'Why have you always enough to eat and drink, clothes to wear, and a house to live in, love all around you, every kind of care and tenderness when you are sick, power to do everything you want for your children, power to spend money on your amusements – even on your luxuries? Does all this make you better? More thoughtful? more unselfish? Do you remember all the time that it comes from God? Here is a contrast. During the terrible weather we had to give our infants hot milk and buns every day. At first they hated the milk and would not take it, and cried out for strong black tea. Fancy 300 little children – babies almost – hating milk.'

Till the veil of death hid him from the eyes of men Dolling never forgot the little children at Poplar, to whom he had been sent to minister.

Serious as the hurt had been to his foot, he finished his preaching, promising to rest after Easter, and place himself in the hands of his doctors.

On Easter Sunday night, March 30, he preached his last sermon to his own people at St. Saviour's Church and went straight off after the service to stay at his sister's house in Philbeach Gardens, Earl's Court. He would not admit that he was seriously ill, but simply said: 'On Easter Monday I am going to put myself in the Doctor's hand and he is going to put me perfectly right; in fact, I think there is nothing the matter with me now.'

But he delivered his message to Poplar, and after April 13 the people there saw his face no more.

Only five weeks later the body of Robert Dolling was brought to St. Saviour's Church, and placed before the altar before the final journey to Woking.

For a week or two after leaving Poplar, the medical care, and nursing, the good food, the better air, and above all, the rest seemed to promise recovery. Then the Incumbent of Berkeley Chapel, Mayfair, gave Dolling permission to preach there every Sunday morning during the London season, and of course, to take the collection. Ill as he was, Dolling could not refuse such a tempting offer – the proceeds would mean so much for Poplar.

He preached on April 13, and, despite the warnings of the doctor, preached again the following Sunday morning. No one who was present will forget the sermon on April 20. It was during the time of negotiations for peace between Lord Kitchener and the Boer Generals. 'We do not pray enough these days,' Dolling said in the middle of the sermon. 'We must pray for peace, if we really want it. Let us all kneel down now, and pray God for peace in South Africa;' and the fashionable congregation knelt.

These sermons were a great effort and a last effort, for the strength of Robert Dolling was spent. His wonderful vitality made the thought of death so alien; he had been ill so often before, and had always pulled through. One never thought of him as a sick man, even when he was quite out of health. From April 20 he was sinking, but we could not think that the sickness was mortal.

No more preaching was possible at Berkeley Chapel, no more parochial anxieties must trouble him. For three weeks he lay in his room at Philbeach Gardens looking out on the trees, and day by day his strength grew less. Some internal trouble afflicted him; the excessive stoutness which compelled him to preach sitting down meant disease. There was weakness of the heart too, and the cold weather was all against recovery. Yet he managed even then to see a party of boys from Shrewsbury School, who, not knowing his serious state, came to consult him concerning a school mission.

The cleverest and most experienced doctors in London could do no more for him, the devoted nursing of his sisters could not save him. Pneumonia set in; there came a few days of unconsciousness, and some talk in the unconsciousness of 'souls to be saved,' and then on the afternoon of Thursday, May 15, while his sister, Miss Elise Dolling, who had shared so much of his life-work, held his hand, the soul of Robert Radclyffe Dolling passed beyond the frontiers of earth.

Dolling was dead.

The silver cord that bound his spirit to the earth was loosed, the golden bowl of his great heart was broken.

The day's work was finished.

Many times, in the gray streets of Poplar, women and children asked anxiously how 'the Father' was, and now, when they heard that he was dead turned tearfully away. Strong men went home in silence that night with a strange lump in the throat, and the feeling that something had gone out of their lives.

It was hard to think of Dolling dead; he had always stood for Life – Life had been his gospel – and he was only fifty-one. Death was never in his preaching – to bring Life and Life more abundant to people was his message. Death never entered into his plans, though he had stood by the bedside of many a dying soul, and said brave words of comfort to many mourners. In those last weeks he never spoke of death, nor made arrangements for putting his earthly affairs in order. He had walked with his God from childhood, and his God was with him when he passed through the valley of the shadow of death. That was enough. He had no property to leave, for the family estate in Ireland which stood in his name had never been a source of personal income to him, and no will was made. For all his 'children' whom he had tended so many years, in the name of God, God would provide. He died, without thought of death, for his God was the Resurrection and the Life. And he died penniless, empty of this world's goods, rich only in the love of those for whom he laid down his life. It was the harvest for which he had sown. The honours, titles, riches of the world Dolling had never sought; the love he had scattered so lavishly on his friends, on his 'children' throughout the world, he reaped ten thousandfold.

The body of Father Dolling was carried from 88, Philbeach Gardens, into St. Cuthbert's Church, which stands near by, on the Monday evening, Vespers of the Dead was sung, and all night long men and women kept watch in the silent church. A Requiem Mass was sung next morning, and West-End folks, to whom Dolling had brought the knowledge of a wider, nobler, and more generous life than that of selfish ease, and whose love he had enlisted in the cause of earth's poor, paid their last tribute sadly to the dead.

In the afternoon the funeral procession moved from St. Cuthbert's through the crowded London streets to Poplar.

Again the service of the dead were recited, and St. Saviour's Church was crowded that Tuesday night. The coffin was placed in the chancel, candles burned round it, flowers covered it, and all that night, too, men and women watched by it till dawn. It was but, the dust of Father Dolling that rested in the coffin, but 'that dust was once a man,' and so human are we that we cling to the outwards symbols that still mark the form of those whom we love, and must, whatever our religion, do honour to the dead. It is not for the sake of the dead, but because of our own weakness, which craves some outward expression for the grief that is gnawing our hearts, that funeral services must be held. When the heroes whom we have loved and followed are taken from us, when the visible cord of some strong affection has been snapped by death, it is so hard to mourn in silence. It is useless to talk of 'superstition,' to prate of philosophy. We *know* the dead are at rest, but our own hearts are breaking, and will not be comforted. The visible and external play so great a part in our lives that we cannot dismiss them in the hour of mourning. Only those of Dolling's friends who were kept in far-off places from these last common acts of reverence for the dead whom we loved, know the bitterness of those lonely days of sorrow.

Dolling was at rest in the last sleep of man, but we were still left to our work though our friend was gone. If only we could have looked once more on his face, only shown by our presence how much we loved him, learnt in the common grief to forget our own, there would have been comfort. But while the Psalms of mourning were sung in St. Saviour's Church, while priests said solemn Requiem Masses, men and women in lonely country places in England and abroad, many soldiers in barracks, sailors at sea, and sick people in hospitals, could only bear their grief in silence. Perhaps a day may come when humanity will look less to the outward things, and live more in the invisible. Some strong souls now are weaned from the external, and find eternal life in the unseen. But through the ages the race has not yet learned to dispense with outward tokens, and craves in its joy and sorrow for symbols and sacraments. For the satisfaction of the human heart of the Christian Church gives its sacraments, and gives some measure of relief to the multitude who, never calling themselves Christian, still know the intolerable burden of solitary grief. The Infinite will not judge man harshly for the weakness that cries for help, and only the churlish would take away from his brother the expression of sorrow that brings comfort to the mourner. So often reason and philosophy leave us comfortless in the hour of distress, and we turn again as little children to the symbols that bring relief.

All religions minister to man in the presence of death, and in this twentieth century humanity still makes offerings for the dead, still makes public procession in mourning, and pays common honour to the dead whom it loves.

The Catholic who finds in the Mass the expression of his worship of the Infinite turns to the Requiem Mass in the hour of bereavement. With the Protestant the prayer-meeting, the hymn-singing, and the sermon are the expression of worship, and so his funeral service takes that form. The secularist, in the same spirit, has his public meeting and oration. In each case the human heart finds solace in the common outward mourning.

So on that Wednesday morning in May priests said their Mass in St. Saviour's Church from five o'clock till half-past eight. The Rev. B. E. Waud, the Rev. A. J. S. Melville, the Rev. C. E. Osborne and others who had ministered with Dolling at the altar, offered the simple Christian sacrifice – it was all they could do. At nine the children came – Dolling always believed it was good for children to come to Mass – and at ten o'clock the Rev. J. Elwes, who was with Dolling at Salisbury Theological College, and who was left in charge of the parish sang the solemn Requiem Mass. The church was crowded till there was no room left, and many people were unable to get inside. At the entrance to the chancel throughout the service stood two soldiers, with arms reversed – two of Dolling's old boys. Scattered about the church were many soldiers in uniform and many clergymen. Those who had worked with him for so long, his sisters and their friends, had a great multitude of fellow-mourners. The High-Church societies to which Dolling belonged sent their representatives. The Mayor of Poplar and Mrs. Crooks came to pay their last respects to their friend and neighbour, and the rest of that congregation was made up of men and women not famous in the world, not distinguished – obscure people mostly, who only knew that 'the Father' was their friend, and that he was dead. The last rites of the Catholic Church were performed, the coffin was censed and sprinkled with holy water, and *Nunc Dimittis* was sung.

One by one the mourners filed up the church to take farewell of the body as it lay in the chancel, while the church bell tolled. Quietly and without any confusion they passed the coffin that held the dead.

At twelve o'clock the Bishop of London read the opening sentences of the Burial Service in the Prayer-Book. A psalm was sung, the Bishop of Stepney read the lesson from St. Paul's Epistle to the Corinthians, and then the Bishop of London gave a short address. Less than four years ago he had instituted Father Dolling to the living, and now he bore witness that Dolling had been a true and faithful priest. He recalled how at a Church Congress at which they had been present, the burden of Dolling's speech to the clergy was, 'Do you love your people?' When everybody else had given a man up, it was always said, 'Will Dolling take him?' Dr. Ingram finished with the prayer that eternal peace might rest upon him, that eternal light might shine upon him, and that his untiring spirit might yet find work beyond the veil.

A hymn was sung, 'Now the labourer's task is o'er,' the Bishop gave the Blessing, and the service in the church was over.

Six soldiers whom Dolling had befriended – a colour-sergeant of the Grenadier Guards, a sergeant of the Royal Marines, and sergeant of the Royal Artillery, two privates in the East Surrey Regiment, and one from Kneller Hall – bore the coffin down the church to the open hearse outside, and then the procession slowly passed through streets densely crowded with mourners. The shops had their shutters up, the blinds were down in all the houses, Poplar was mourning for 'the Father' who had lived among his people, and had passed from them.

The train took the coffin and its mourners to Woking, and more than one hundred people from St. Agatha's were at the grave-side. They, not of the great and mighty of the earth, had travelled from Portsmouth to see the last resting-place of 'the Father.' Many of Dolling's friends were there – Father Stanton, more than ten years Dolling's senior; Dr. Burge, the headmaster of Winchester; several Winchester masters; old Wykehamists; the Rev. E. W. Sergeant, who had worked at St. Agatha's with Dr. Linklater in the early days of the Mission; certain army officers; and a great company whose names and lives were written on the dead man's heart.

In the beautiful private burial-ground of St. Alban's, Holborn, in Woking Cemetery, surrounded by fir-trees, and close by the grave of Maconochie, they placed the body in the ground.

The Bishop of Stepney read the last part of the Burial Service at the open grave, and spoke a few words, commending to their prayers those whom Robert Dolling had left behind – his sisters, his people at Portsmouth and Poplar, his soldier and sailors all over the world, the Winchester boys, all the weary and tired ones, the desolate and broken who had turned to him and had never turned in vain.

In silence the mourners filed past the grave, and slowly and quietly retraced their steps.

In the warm sunlight, at the time when the lilacs bloom and the thrush gives his song, the body of Robert Dolling was laid to rest. Peacefully, amid the firs of Surrey, in that quiet corner of the earth, his body sleeps. But the spirit of Robert Dolling, is with us still, inspiring and encouraging all who battle for the poor and oppressed, bidding us to love the brotherhood, urging us to live as sons of God. No man can tell all the work that Dolling did, no man can measure the fulness of his love. The love that Robert Dolling shed upon the earth has not passed into the grave, but remains a moving force in the world. His God was Love. Nothing was holier than love in Dolling's eyes, and because the God of this earth is a living God, so Dolling lives also – lives in every movement of love in his 'children.'

Peacefully may his poor, tired body sleep! Within it lived a man who in our day and generation showed us what love meant, and in so doing showed us God Himself.

'Greater love hath no man than this, that a man lay down his life for his friends.

CHAPTER XIII

A NOTE ON DOLLING'S 'METHODS'

Dolling was a great personality, a very complete man. Every aspect of human life interested him keenly, his sympathies were universal.

'People who have hearts are simple in all their ways,' Balzac wrote, and Dolling's large-heartedness accounts for the wonderful sympathy and frankness of his life. The explanation of Dolling's influence is not in his 'magnetic' personality, but in his great love for his fellows – a love that made all insincerity or affectation impossible, and caused him to be perfectly frank and *en rapport* with every man he met.

Sometimes people talk about Dolling's success as a clergyman, and discuss his methods, his dancing-classes, or his ritualism. Such talk is all beside the mark. There is only one way to achieve success as Dolling achieved it – to love; and as that love deepens and burns more ardently, so will a natural frankness and simplicity arise that will enable its possessor to walk through the world with dignity and ease, giving and receiving blessing as he goes, and comforting pain and disappointment without dismay. Without a great love for mankind, without a heart that is touched by the joys and sorrows around us, none of

'Dolling's methods' will be profitable. Frankness without an innate sympathy is apt to become impertinence, and to degenerate into that familiarity that breeds contempt. Where love is, there is respect – ay, and though we love the least respectable or respected, still there is something divine in the object of our love, some likeness still to the God, in Whose Image man is made, that demands our reverence. And because many clergymen and other religious workers lack this sympathy, and have no heart aglow with love for their kind, their studied plainness of speech and affected ease of manner often appear merely vulgar, and not at all commendable. 'Dolling's methods' are eminently the right thing for – a Dolling. The parish priest whose sympathies are restricted, who is conscious that his heart does not burn or ache with joy or sorrow for his neighbours, had much better not attempt the social work that Dolling carried out so successfully. Let the love come first, let the heart be there, and then there will be no need to affect an interest in one's neighbour's doings, or to display a concern, so obviously well meant, but so obviously unreal, for their welfare. Instinctively the heart will prompt the right word to be spoken if we love; and the stronger the love for mankind, the simpler will be our talk and conduct.

As Dolling was frank and simple in his dealings with men because of the great love he bore mankind, so in his dealings with his God was he equally simple and frank, because here, too, his heart went out in love. He was as a little child in religion. His God was his Father, to whom he told with perfect openness all his wants, and in whom he trusted with entire confidence. It was quite natural for

Dolling to pray for 'a fine day to-morrow, because it's our Sunday-school outing,' for 'a job to be found' for one of his out-or-work friends, for all the spiritual and physical needs of his 'children.' God knew best how the petition should be fulfilled; there was never any thought of questioning God's goodness or wisdom if the Sunday-school outing was spoilt by a wet day, and if the job was not forthcoming for a man out of work. As he prayed for all his friends living, so he naturally went on praying for them when they were dead. Were the not his friends still? He couldn't explain with any theological nicety what good these prayers did, for all his religion was from the fulness of his heart but he could not help praying. It was his simple belief in God, untouched by any controversies or speculations of the hour, that drew him to the piety of the Nonconformists.

Largeness of heart is the key, then, to Dolling's character. It gave him that charm of manner that attracted so mixed a multitude to him. A glance at the list of his friends who form the Memorial Committee will show how men of widely different habits and thought were drawn to him. It made him at home in any society of men and women. It stamped his preaching and his public speaking with a sincerity that was irresistible.

At the same time, there was no feminine weakness with this great tenderness of heart, but the strength and vigour of full-grown manhood. In the more God-like of the race are always combined the higher characteristics of both sexes, the sympathy and tenderness of the woman with the strength and courage of the man; and mankind ceases to think of the sex of these rare souls, but hails them as saints, heroes, demi-gods. They are not non-sexual, but bisexual; and of this company, at the head of which is Christ of Galilee, was Robert Dolling. His tenderness was the tenderness of a woman, but it was never feminine; and he would fight for his 'children,' for the oppressed and over-burdened, as a mother fights for her offspring, and fight to some purpose, as we have shown. So strong was this combination of strength and tenderness in Dolling that he was quite as much in his element when a contest was on foot as he was when he was binding up the wounds of some poor soul in his study or in the confessional. And here, again, those who want to adopt 'Dolling's methods' must be careful that they cultivate the strength as well as the tenderness of his character.

When shams, cant, pretences, conventions that destroyed the spirit to preserve the letter, and humbug generally, stood before him. Dolling struck at them bravely, and enjoyed it. He was no respecter of persons where injustice or humbug was concerned, and the whole bench of Anglican Bishops, lawn sleeves, palaces, seats in the House of Lords, and all, could never hinder Dolling from speaking his mind freely on episcopal shortcomings. He resembled Charles Dickens in his opposition to and dislike of the pompous official, and twice in his ministry of nineteen years he threw up his work – at Mile End and Portsmouth – sooner than submit to what he considered episcopal ill-treatment. It was because the Church of England claimed so much, and its ministers were so often ineffective, that Dolling spoke more harshly of his brother clergy than of any other body of men; and this impatience had its roots in his simplicity of mind. Why couldn't they all be natural and without pretensions as he was? It was not the fallen clerics, the men who have brought discredit on themselves and their profession by over-indulgence, who provoked Dolling's impatience – for them he had healing sympathy and compassion; it was the entirely respectable High-Church clergyman, strong in assurance of his power to bind and loose, and of his apostolical succession – the typical Pharisee of to-day thanking God that he is not as these dissenters or Roman Catholics – of whom Dolling spoke sharply and contemptuously. 'It make me oftentimes sick at heart to hear the way in which the newly-ordained, strong in the orthodoxy of his High-Church collar and of his grasp of doctrine, speaks of these Nonconformist class-leaders, at whose feet he is unworthy to sit.' So Dolling declared in one of his sermons for the Christian Social Union in 1895. The men of humble faith in God, and the men of broken and contrite hearts, Dolling recognised as his brothers; for the self-satisfied and the righteous he had no words of comfort. And in this matter, perhaps, he had but assimilated the teaching of the life of his Master.

What else can we say of Robert Radclyffe Dolling? 'People who have hearts are simple in all their ways.' More than anything I can say these words explain his character. His God was Love, his Master the Friend of publicans and sinners. A thousand and one acts of simple brotherly charity are recalled as we think of the years in East London and Portsmouth; the natural eloquence of a preacher who 'saw things clearly, and who saw them whole,' is remembered; the stanch friend who loved men and women for what they were and not for the opinions they expressed, is again before us. And now that Robert Dolling has passed from the shadow in which men walk and disquiet themselves in vain, passed to the rest that remains for the people of God, their still lives on in all who knew him well and loved him some portion of his spirit. In the fashionable West-End churches where he preached, at Winchester, and in the day-schools at Poplar, in prisons, workhouses, and hospitals to whose inmates he ministered, on ships at sea, and in army barracks, amongst the outcast men and women of our streets – in all these places has the spirit of Robert Dolling moved. And the fashionable society woman and the harlot, the public-school man and the child of the national school, the soldier and the sailor, the thief and the pauper, have all felt the moving of that spirit, and their hearts have been quickened at his presence. No one could enumerate to the full the names of Father Dolling's 'children,' and in all these 'children' there is a wider charity and a stronger courage because they walked with him.

And so the influence of Dolling lives on in the world, and must live on even when his name is forgotten. The body of the man we loved is at rest at Woking, all the books and records of his life will crumble to dust, but the love in which Dolling lived, the love which he transmitted to his 'children,' grows larger every day; for it is the charity of God, the spirit that transcends the ways of earth, the priceless heritage of mortals, the very eternal life.

AFTERWORDS

THE MEMORIAL

The testimony of the press to Father Dolling's work was remarkable. At Portsmouth and Poplar his activities were often the subject of appreciative newspaper articles, and after his death papers representing every shade of political and religious opinion had but one common verdict on the nobility of Dolling's character. There is no need to repeat this testimony of the press, but the following quotation must be made from an article in the *Pilot*, written by a Roman Catholic priest who knew Dolling intimately for twenty-five years, who, to a large extent, owed his faith to him, and who never at any time regarded his submission to Rome as humanly probable,' because it throws real light on Dolling's theological perceptions.

'Incredible as it may sound to Protestants who looked upon him as a Romanizer of the extremest type, he was, in spite of his easy adoption of nearly the whole system of Catholic doctrine, and practice, an Evangelical to the backbone; that is to say, his whole interest was in the saving of those individual souls – and they were thousands – with whom he came in contact, and not in any ecclesiastical system for its own sake. He cared as little for theology and scholarship as did St. Francis or John Wesley, and it was because he discovered by intuition and experiment that Catholic beliefs and practices were efficacious for the sole end he cared about that he adopted them fearlessly, without much deference to Bishops or Articles. For the same reason he took over as boldly, and to the scandal of ecclesiastical *dilettanti*, such elements of Methodism as by their efficacy with the multitude had proved their right to survive.... *Sacramenta propter homines*, the priest for the people, and not the people for the priest, was a Catholic principle that had taken deep root in a soul governed as his was by a passionate devotion to the multitudes; and it was because he fancied that an inversion of this principle was not merely a local or transitory accident, but an inherent characteristic of the Church of Rome, that his affections remained alienated from us to the end.'

There was less testimony from the pulpit than from the press, but, of course, a Poplar and Portsmouth, and at St. Albans, Holborn, there were eloquent tributes to the dead; and in at least two Nonconformist chapels – the Lake Road Baptist Church, Landport, and the Congregational Church, Baldock, Herts – Memorial Services were held at the time of Father Dolling's funeral.

A committee was formed very soon after Dolling's death to raise some memorial. Amongst the members of this committee are men of the most widely different opinions, and the fact that they are here working together is no small indication of the catholicity of Dolling's friendships. After due consideration the committee came to the following decision: (1) To provide for the comfort or Mr. Dolling's two sisters, without whose devoted labours it would have been impossible for their brother to have carried on his work, and who were dependent on him; (2) to provide a small Convalescent Home for Working Girls; (3) that the Misses Dolling should be asked to undertake the management of this home; (4) that the benefits of the Home should, in the first instance, be for those recommended by the authorities of St. Agatha's, Landport and St. Saviour's, Poplar, the scenes of Mr. Dolling's chief labours.

Money is still wanted for the second of these proposals and subscriptions and donations may be sent either to the Rev. J. H. R. Abbott, at Seghill Vicarage, Dudley, R.S.O., Northumberland, or to Mr. W. M. Walter, Manager, London and County Bank, 52, East India Dock Road, London, E., the envelopes marked 'Dolling Memorial Fund.'

No costly monument in marble is suggested, but this little Convalescent Home might well stand to hand down from generation to generation the name of Robert Radclyffe Dolling.

THE END